Therapy Games for Teens & Middle School Students

150+ Fun Activities to Improve Social Skills, Build Self-Esteem, Regulate Emotions and Develop Coping Skills. (Master Your Emotions Workbook)

By

Kardas Publishing

© **Copyright 2022 by Kardas Publishing - All rights reserved.**

Without the prior written permission of the Publisher, no part of this publication may be stored in a retrieval system, replicated, or transferred in any form or medium, digital, scanning, recording, printing, mechanical, or otherwise, except as permitted under 1976 United States Copyright Act, section 107 or 108. Permission concerns should be directed to the publisher's permission department.

Legal Notice

This book is copyright protected. It is only to be used for personal purposes. Without the author's or publisher's permission, you cannot paraphrase, quote, copy, distribute, sell, or change any part of the information in this book.

Disclaimer Notice

This book is written and published independently. Please keep in mind that the material in this publication is solely for educational and entertaining purposes. All efforts have provided authentic, up-to-date, trustworthy, and comprehensive information. There are no express or implied assurances. The purpose of this book's material is to assist readers in having a better understanding of the subject matter. The activities, information, and exercises are provided solely for self-help information. This book is not intended to replace expert psychologists, legal, financial, or other guidance. If you require counseling, please get in touch with a qualified professional.

By reading this text, the reader accepts that the author will not be held liable for any damages, indirectly or directly, experienced due to the use of the information included herein, particularly, but not limited to, omissions, errors, or inaccuracies. As a reader, you are accountable for your decisions, actions, and consequences.

A FREE PRINTABLE GIFT TO OUR READERS!

Print it at home!

Get FREE, unlimited access to it and all our new books by joining our community!

SCAN WITH YOUR CAMERA TO JOIN!

CONTENTS

INTRODUCTION	13
PART-I	16
SOCIAL SKILLS DEVELOPMENT	16
CHAPTER 1	21
BETTER COMMUNICATION SKILLS	21
Card Pieces	23
Listen and Draw	25
Communication Origami	26
Guess the Emotion	27
Telephone Activity	28
Listener and Talker	29
Memory Test	30
Clap and Follow	31
Stack the Deck	32
Silent Movie	33
Eye-to-Eye Game	34
The Guessing Game	35
End of the Word—Beginning of the Next Game	36
Silent Snack Activity	37
CHAPTER 2	38
BETTER RELATIONSHIPS DEVELOPMENT SKILLS	38
Sharing	39
Cooperating	41
Listening	42

- Respecting Personal Space 45
- Using Manners 47
- Developing Positive Relationships 49
- Compliment Circle Activity 52
- My Family 55
- Family Relationships 57
- Shared Qualities 59
- Relationships: Take Charge 61
- Character Relationship 62
- Healthy Relationship 64
- Games for Developing Healthy Relationships 67

CHAPTER 3 70
INCREASING HAPPINESS SKILLS 70

- Playing Outside and Practice Positivity 72
- Train Your Brain 73
- Install Happiness Triggers 76
- Write it Down 77
- Practice Gratitude 79
- Have High but Achievable Expectations 80
- Teach Self-Control 81
- Freeze Dance 82
- Things that make me Happy Activity 84
- The Feeling of the Day Activity 85
- When I am Feeling Happy Worksheet 86
- Happy and Mad 87
- Happy Words 88

My Happy Sheet 89

My Feel Happier Flower 90

CHAPTER 4 91
GREATER EFFICIENCY & CREATIVITY SKILLS 91

First Things First 93

Break It Down 93

Time Tracking 93

Watch for Weariness 94

Encourage 94

Give Them a Space 94

Self-Reliance 94

Participate in Healthy Competition 95

Encourage Confidence 95

Creative Drawing 96

Beach Story 97

Creative Writing Sheet 98

Imagining Pet Creativity 99

Time Machine Fun Activity 100

Games to Develop Creativity Skills 101

PART-II 104
SKILLS FOR BUILDING SELF-ESTEEM 104

CHAPTER 5 106
CHALLENGING NEGATIVE BELIEFS 106

Understand Your Thought Patterns 106

Start a Thought Diary 109

Ability-Talk, Effort-Talk, Self-Talk 111

Cultivate Self Awareness 112

- Practice Self-Love 114
- Dispute the Irrational Thoughts 115
- Ways to Challenge Negative Thoughts 116
- All or Nothing Thinking 117
- Overcoming Negative Thoughts 118
- Automatic Negative Thoughts 119
- Changing Negative Thoughts 120
- Challenging Negative Thoughts 121
- Gratitude 122
- Mindfulness Activities and Games 125

CHAPTER 6 127
IDENTIFYING THE POSITIVE 127

- Focus on Solutions, Not on Problems 129
- Replace Your Negative Thoughts with Positive Thoughts ... 131
- Repeat Affirmations 133
- Do Not Take Anything Too Personally 134
- Keep it Positive 135
- Positively Wonderful 137
- Positive Thinking Please 138
- Optimism 139
- Optimism Sheet 2 140
- Positive Affirmation 141
- My Daily Affirmations 143
- 10 Minutes to Recognize Good Stuff 144
- Mindfulness Activities and Games 145

CHAPTER 7 147
IMPROVING PHYSICAL HEALTH 147

Set A Goal 149

Get Creative 150

Make Exercise a Family Priority 153

Jumping Jacks Game 154

Physical Activity through Games 155

Fill Up a Balloon and Don't Let It Touch the Ground Game 156

Developing Core Stability Games 157

Healthy Habits 158

Healthy Habits Game 160

Physical Activity 161

Staying Healthy 162

Health and Wellness Check 163

Self-Care Activity 164

CHAPTER 8 166
BECOMING MORE ASSERTIVE 166

Building A Healthy Self-Perception 168

Self-Talk for Assertiveness 169

Planning What You Are Talking About 170

Self-Evaluation for Assertiveness 171

Assertive Talk 173

5 Exercises for Assertiveness 175

Passive, Aggressive, and Assertive Communication 176

Passive, Aggressive, and Assertive 177

Asking Help 179

Standing Up for Yourself 181

Meeting New People 181

Making Mistakes 181

PART-III 182
EMOTIONS REGULATION SKILLS 182

CHAPTER 9 184
STRESS MANAGEMENT SKILLS 184

Talk About Your Problems 185
Go Easy on Yourself 186
Eliminate Your Triggers 187
Causes of Stress 189
Stress and My Body 190
That Stressed Me Out 191
My Stress Triggers 192
Recognizing Stress 194
My Stressed-Out List 195
Stress Management 197
My Stress Management Plan 198
Stress Management Mindful Exercises 199
Stress Relief Games 202

CHAPTER 10 203
DEPRESSION AND ANXIETY MANAGEMENT SKILLS . 203

Socialize 204
Keep your Body and Mind Healthy 205
What Bugs Me? 206
Depression and My Body 207
Depression Coping Plan 208
Introduction to Anxiety 209
Anxiety Breakdown 210
My Anxiety Levels 211

My Social Anxiety 212
Anxiety vs. Truth 213
Mindfulness Exercises for Anxiety Management 214
Mindfulness Exercises for Depression Management 216

CHAPTER 11 218
ANGER AND MOOD DISORDERS MANAGEMENT SKILL 218

Aim for Regulation, Not Repression 219
Identify What You're Feeling 219
Accept Your Emotions 220
Give Yourself Some Space 220
Anger Map 221
My Anger Triggers 222
Anger Exploration 223
I Feel Mad Today 224
Anger Journal 225
How Anger Feels 226
Anger Meter 227
When I Feel Angry 228
Feeling Zones 229
What are you Feeling Today? 231
When I Feel Sad 232
My Emotions Wheel 233
Mindful Exercises 235
Mood Lifting Games 236

CHAPTER 12: WORRY AND FEAR MANAGEMENT SKILLS 238

Stay in the Present Moment 239

Take Small Acts of Bravery 239
Plan Worry Time 240
My Top 5 Worries 241
My Worry Clouds 243
A Peek Inside My Mind 244
Facing Fears 245
Getting to Know My Emotions 246
My Fears 247
Fear Crushing 248
Overcoming Fear Questionnaire 250
Mindfulness Exercise 252

PART-IV 253
DEVELOPING COPING SKILLS 253
CHAPTER 13 255
COPING SKILLS WORKSHEETS AND ACTIVITIES 255

Developing Coping Skills/Resilience 256
Coping Skills Bingo 258
Picking Good Coping Skills 260
Coping Skills Challenges 261
If I Didn't Care 262
Coping Skills Brainstorm 263
Coping Skills Assessment 264
Coping Skills Anywhere 266
I Can Cope 267
Coping with Feelings 268
Roll a Coping Skill 269
Coping Skill Wheel 270

Coping Skill Word Search Game 271

I am Lucky 272

The End Note..274

INTRODUCTION

Teens are developing in a changing world. People worldwide are forced to adapt to unanticipated changes in their lives and employment due to technology, migration, climate change, and conflict. Children need to be able to obtain opportunities and overcome obstacles if they are to keep up with their lives. They need skills and education to develop a love of learning, find fulfilling employment, make wise judgments, and actively participate in their communities.

Life skills are "the capacities for adaptive and good conduct that enable individuals to deal successfully with the requirements and obstacles of everyday life. Teenagers must develop their social and emotional abilities as they learn to be independent. These include helpful interpersonal and psychosocial abilities, such as: resolving issues, communicating clearly, making sensible choices, thinking clearly and critically, being understanding toward others, cultivating wholesome relationships, and self-management.

Parents and teachers should discuss the responsibilities that fall under their purview. Keeping this in mind, parents and teachers cannot intervene directly in some basic skills, such as: domestic duties, arranging meetings, emergencies, emotional regulation skills etc. Teachers can express their concerns about such skills at parent-teacher conferences, though.

"Therapy Games for Teens and Middle School" consists of four parts having different types of life skills for teens, middle school children, parents and teachers. The chapters in each part focuses on skills that kids must learn to transition into adulthood and how you as a teacher or parent may teach them.

While talking about different life skills, emotions regulation is important and basic life skill that kids need to learn in order to avoid stress and mental issues that come with the growing. A part of this book is dedicated to emotional skill learning. A teenager's life can only go so far with pure talent and aptitude. They also need to learn how to control their emotions. Emotions can be varied and intricate. It's helpful to be able to empathize or deal with failure. Teens will be better able to handle setbacks if they manage their temper. For a teen, controlling their anxiety can lead to new opportunities outside their comfort zone. There are many good strategies to handle unpleasant emotions discussed in the book.

Teenagers must also learn how to defend themselves on the other end of the spectrum. A part of this book is also written on some basic communication skills to make children realize that aggressiveness and assertiveness are not the same things. Teens can thrive if they understand the differences! This life skills book aims to integrate life skills like emotional regulation, communication, social life skills etc. into classroom or household environments.

This book will also highlight some strategies for teachers and parents. This book will help you to understand that there is a potential in your teen that they will fail to identify if you force them to complete a task they don't want to. Refrain from rushing into things. While it's always crucial to have your child's back, sometimes kids must fail to succeed. Before you assist, give them time to sort things out independently. You could just be surprised.

This is the book that not only assists you as a parent or teacher but also your teens who are struggling to live a fulfilling life.

Then what are you waiting for?

Keep reading, explore skills and teach through worksheets, exercises, activities, games, and mindfulness techniques.

PART-I

SOCIAL SKILLS DEVELOPMENT

Hi Parents/Teachers!

You've likely read numerous books on how essential social skills are for teens. It might be challenging to progress when you don't fully comprehend social skills and how to work on them.

People find it challenging to master social. Many of our readers believe that they were the only ones who didn't develop social skills in high school because they were absent from the class where everyone else did.

It's clear that there wasn't a class like that, and you're not the only person who finds it difficult to comprehend social skills. We'll examine social skills in this part, including what they are, why they're crucial (and challenging), and strategies for developing them.

Social success is facilitated through interpersonal communication techniques. They allow you to properly communicate with others and decipher their verbal and nonverbal cues.

One method of psychology divides social skills into five categories: empathy, self-control, self-advocacy, and cooperation.

Cooperation, which includes negotiation and persuasion, is how successfully you collaborate with other people to complete a task.

Your ability to start **social engagements**, such as introducing yourself to others, demonstrates your assertiveness.

By exercising self-control, you can healthily manage your emotions, for as, by controlling your temper.

Understanding how your activities affect other people and acting responsibly are key components of **responsibility**.

Therapy Games for Teens & Middle School

Understanding how others might be experiencing and being able to put oneself in their situation are two characteristics of **empathy**. It serves as a gauge of social perception.

Having social skills can be challenging because there aren't any set rules. Contrary to arithmetic or physics, repeating the same action will not produce the same outcome. Accurately interpreting another person's thoughts and feelings is frequently the foundation of social skills.

It might be beneficial to consider social skills in terms of their three fundamental components—understanding feelings, including your own, comprehending the social setting, and exhibiting appropriate social behavior.

For instance, if your teen observes someone crying, empathy enables him to understand that they may be distressed and need comforting. Your kid can evaluate how well they know someone by using their knowledge of the social setting. Hugging or giving them a tissue could be the appropriate social action.

But...

What makes social skills important?

Every element of your life, including finding a good friend, how much money you make, and even how healthful you are, can be impacted by your social skills. Here are a few of the most significant advantages of social skill development.

More Effective Connections

Establishing positive partnerships requires social skills. Our social abilities enable us to comprehend the feelings and needs of our friends, relatives, and coworkers.

Improved Communication

The key to social skills is communication. People with good social skills can interpret another person's body language and comprehend more of what they are saying. Additionally, they can establish rapport, which makes it simpler for people to be open with them.

Increasing Career Opportunities

Greater social skills are also associated with better professional opportunities. According to studies, persons with stronger social skills have more successful professions. They have greater life and professional satisfaction, which makes it simpler for them to remain motivated.

Feeling Better

Socially adept people are typically happier than those who are not. This is mainly because those with strong social skills can develop a large number and variety of friendships. These relationships support you when times are tough and help you meet your emotional requirements.

Better Academic Results

Children who have stronger social skills often perform better academically. Socially adept students may be expected to do better by teachers, which leads to a self-fulfilling prophecy. Socially adept children also frequently exhibit fewer disruptive behaviors, giving them more study time and energy.

Avoiding Loneliness

Being more socially adept can help you avoid loneliness. You can develop stronger friendships without the need for strong social skills. Additionally, they offer you the courage to approach those close to you when you feel lonely.

Improved Health

Better social skills enhance more than simply your emotional wellbeing. Your physical and emotional health can both benefit from it.

For instance, research indicates that bulimic patients have inferior social skills and support systems. Strong social skills are said to assist people in creating support networks that safeguard their social and mental health.

Additionally, having good social skills can help you receive better medical care. This can involve being able to convey your symptoms, receiving an urgent consultation when you need one, and having doctors believe your evaluation of your needs.

Thus, this part will solely focus on developing social skills in teens. This part consists of four chapters. There are some descriptive exercises, some tips to develop that social skill and some worksheets have been given. Teens can do these worksheets and exercises by themselves while parents and teachers can use tips to develop social skills.

Let's move forward to chapters.

CHAPTER 1
BETTER COMMUNICATION SKILLS

Hey Teens!

The tools in this chapter offer you the chance to learn more about successful communication, help direct your interactions with others, and enhance your communication skills. These include group exercises, games, and individual activities. They will help you improve, become more efficient, and be positive and good speakers with those who matter the most.

But...

What's the importance of these games, exercises, and activities? Do they truly have that much impact or importance? Do we need to improve our communication skills when it looks like we do so already?

Imagine Cindy, a thirteen-year-old girl, alone in her classroom. Her peers taunt and neglect her. She behaves differently in social situations. She misinterprets facial expressions and hand movements. She doesn't have anyone to play with during the break. Cindy senses being alone. She struggles to get out of bed in the morning so she can go to school and deal with this social rejection. According to Cindy's case study, the assessment reveals that she struggles to interact with classmates and comprehend how to respond to circumstances. The purpose of the social stories is to equip Cindy with the ability to adapt her social abilities to the demands of a given circumstance. Cindy's daily life has been damaged by her lack of social skills, which has emotionally drained her ability to grow in confidence and self-esteem. Cindy would get the chance to investigate touchy subjects and discover how to assess a solution to a current situation.

So...

How can we improve our communication abilities?

Fortunately, improving communication skills requires a commitment to do so and some work. With a little modification, the following tips, exercises and activities can also be used in any other relationship in your life to assist you in improving communication with your friends and family.

Keep going and you will be a great communicator.

Card Pieces

(Instructions for Parents/Teachers)

This activity is a helpful method to encourage participants to think about various points of view, increase their capacity for empathy, and improve their communication and conflict resolution abilities.

A minimum of three teams of two players should be present, and you also need to have enough playing cards to distribute 4 to 6 cards to each player and 15 minutes to spare.

The activity is as follows:

- Make sure to have card decks equal to your teams. If you have two teams, have two decks.
- Each card deck is divided into four pieces by first shuffling it in half crosswise, then in half again.
- Combine all the components, then distribute the same number of cards into each team's envelope.
- Give an equal number of cards to each team in an envelope.
- Every team has 3 minutes to organize their pieces.
- Allow the teams to begin trading for items after three minutes. Either individually or collectively with their team. Allow each team eight minutes to haggle.
- Count the completed cards from each team as the timer expires. The side with the most cards at the end of the round wins.

Following the activity, you can use the following queries to help lead the discussion:

- Which negotiating tactics were successful? Which were not successful?
- What might they have improved upon?

- What other abilities, such as empathy or active listening, were required?

Listen and Draw

(Instructions for Parents/Teachers)

Playing this game is simple, but "winning" is hard. Participants must pay attention and listen intently.

How to Play?

Give each player a piece of paper and a notepad or pencil as you assemble your group of participants. Inform them that you would give them verbal directions, one step at a time, on how to draw an item.

You could, for instance, order them to:

- Draw a square with 5-inch sides.
- Draw a circle inside the square that precisely fits in the center of the area.
- Cut the circle into four equal pieces by intersecting two lines.

The difficulty of the exercise will increase as you go along; one mistake could cause all subsequent instructions to be misunderstood or applied incorrectly. To guarantee that their drawings are accurate, participants must pay close attention while listening. After reading the instructions, compare the drawings to choose the winner.

Decide what the end work represents for greater participation (e.g., a spider web, a tree).

Communication Origami

(Instructions for Parents/Teachers)

This is an excellent activity to show people that we hear and understand things differently, even when presented with the same information.

This is how it goes:

- Each participant should receive one sheet of plain paper.
- Inform your attendees that you will demonstrate how to bend their bit of paper into an origami form step-by-step.
- Tell your participants that while following instructions, they must keep their eyes and lips shut and are not permitted to look at the material or ask any questions for clarity.
- You should explain to the group how to bend the paper into the desired origami shape.
- After everyone has heard the instructions, ask them to open their eyes and match their shapes with the intended ones.

Each shape is likely a little bit different, as you will discover! Refer to these discussion topics and questions:

- Make the argument that even though you gave everyone the same directions, each paper's shape appears distinct. Why does this matter?
- If the group had been permitted to ask questions or kept their eyes open, do you believe the outcomes would have been better?
- It's difficult to communicate clearly since everyone interprets information differently. For this reason, it's crucial to check for understanding and ask questions to ensure the message is not twisted.

Guess the Emotion

(Instructions for Parents/Teachers)

"Guess the Emotion" is a helpful activity. It entails acting out and assuming emotions, as you might anticipate. This enables all participants to develop empathy skills and better comprehend the reactions of their coworkers or other group members.

To play this entertaining game, follow these instructions:

- Make two teams out of the group.
- A packet of cards with "this emotion (any)" written on them should be placed on a table (or in a box).
- Have a member of Group (A) choose the highest card from the table and pantomime the emotion for the rest of the group. This must be completed within a specific time frame (such as a minute or two).
- Group (A) scores ten points if they properly identify the emotion.
- Have a member of Group (B) act out a feeling now, and assign points accordingly.
- The two groups should alternate getting to act.
- Call time on the acting and guessing after 15 to 20 minutes, then identify the winning team depending on their point total.

Consider awarding the winning team a trophy if your group is very competitive!

Telephone Activity

(Instructions for Parents/Teachers)

This time-tested exercise demonstrates the value of listening and the need to take advantage of any opportunity.

How to proceed?

Divide your team into two equal lines. Whisper a word or brief message to the person at the end of each line, who is on the opposite end, and instruct them to pass it on to one person at a time using just whispers. The phrase or sentence may only be used once.

Play music or start a conversation with participants to provide white noise while they are busy handing the message to the next person waiting. This will make it slightly more challenging but will simulate real-life situations with many distractions.

Have the last person to hear a letter in each line report what they have heard once the messages have reached the end of each line. Next, have the first person to hear each line of the message describe the initial message and contrast it with the message they eventually heard.

Listener and Talker

(Instructions for Parents/Teachers)

Another useful exercise for emphasizing the value of attentive learning and providing participants an opportunity to practice their abilities is the "Listener and Talker" activity.

Split your team into pairs, with one partner taking on the role of the talker and the other taking on the role of the listener. Without naming a location, the talker's task is to express what they desire from a holiday. It is the responsibility of the listener to pay close attention to both what is said and what is not expressed and to show this awareness by their actions.

The listener should summarize the three key factors the talker is considering when loving their holiday after a few moments of active listening. Finally, the audience should try to persuade the speaker to choose a vacation spot. The two should reverse roles and try the practice once more after briefly discussing how well the listener paid attention.

Each participant will have the opportunity to practice speaking about their wants and needs, actively listening, and applying their newly acquired information to comprehend and relate to the speaker.

Memory Test

(Instructions for Parents/Teachers)

The "Memory Test" activity is a fantastic exercise.

This is how it goes:

- Inform participants that you will test their memory by reading them a list of words.
- Tell them to pay close attention since they cannot note down any words. Inform them that you'll test them later to see if any of the terms they can recall.
- After reading over the list of words, divert your audience's attention by talking about something for at least a minute.
- As soon as you are done speaking, ask each participant to write down as many words from the list as they can recall.

A list of somewhat random words will be very challenging for you (and your participants) to remember, especially if there is a pause in time and another conversation between having heard them and remembering them! Connect this and actual listening by stressing how important it is to pay attention to others when talking to you, especially if it's a crucial conversation.

Clap and Follow

(Instructions for Parents/Teachers)

It's a great idea to practice utilizing your body in addition to your voice by participating in the "Clap and Follow" activity.

It operates as follows:

Inform your group that they must focus completely on this game. Give them the following advice:

- Tell them that they should get up when they hear one clap from the captain (you).
- They must hop once in place after the leader claps twice.
- They should rub their bellies when they hear three claps.
- They should immediately do a 360-degree turn after hearing four claps.
- They should pat their heads after five claps.

Start the activity now! Once you have delivered the group each command, begin with one clap, then two, and so on.

Mix it up now! Change between the five distinct directions and quicken your pace. The eliminations start at this point.

Eliminate a player from the game each time they engage in improper action. Continue until just one winner can be determined.

If your group is competitive, you might wish to bring a prize to encourage participation in the activity. It will provide an enjoyable setting for participants to practice nonverbal communication.

Stack the Deck

(Instructions for Parents/Teachers)

A set of playing cards, a blindfold for each player, and some room to walk around are all you need for this activity.

This is how "Stack the Deck" functions:

- After the deck has been shuffled, give one card to each player.
- Tell the players to keep their cards private; nobody should know the color or suit of another player's card.
- Inform the participants that speaking is completely prohibited throughout this activity.
- Tell your participants to form four groups, one for each of the four card suits (hearts, clubs, diamonds, and spades), but to communicate entirely nonverbally.
- Try blindfolding each person and providing the same instructions if you have the opportunity and your players have the will to do so; it makes it much more challenging and time-consuming!
- Once everyone is seated in one of the four groups, have the players line up in order of rank (Ace is the weakest, King is the strongest); once more, they must remain silent and not reveal their cards to anybody during this phase of the activity.

The team that lines up first and correctly wins!

You can always encourage your participants by rewarding the winning team.

This activity will demonstrate how challenging nonverbal communication may be. Still, it will demonstrate to your players that it is feasible and becomes simpler as they become more adept at recognizing one another's nonverbal clues.

Silent Movie

(Instructions for Parents/Teachers)

To properly emphasize the value of effective nonverbal communication, encourage this activity.

- Your participants should be split into two groups. One group will participate in the activity as a scriptwriter, and the other will participate as an actor for the first half. The two groups will trade roles in the second half.

Tell the screenwriters to create a silent film while considering the following:

- Without using words, silent films tell a tale. Starting the scene with the actor performing a clear action, such as housework or rowing a boat, is crucial.
- When a second actor (or numerous actors) enters the scene, the scene must be stopped, and their entry should have a significant impact. Any character, including robbers, salespeople, kids, or even animals, could be the story's subject.
- There must be a physical commotion.
- By the end of the scene, the issue that the commotion has caused must be solved.

Allow the screenwriters some time to draft their script before having the performers perform it. Have the groups exchanged roles after the scene is over.

Eye-to-Eye Game

(Instructions for Teens)

Friends can play this game to practice communication and strengthen their bond—all you need are your eyes!

This is how you do it:

- The friends can seat face-to-face and sufficiently near for hand holding.
- Each partner fixes their gaze squarely on the other.
- Each partner should pause for a moment to acknowledge their current feelings.
- One of the partners brings up a specific topic such as what they have eaten for lunch, or something for which they are grateful.
- While maintaining eye contact, the other partner responds by having a discourse of a similar nature.
- The pair continues to share one item at a time until each person has given at least 3 - 4 times.
- The pair will discuss the experience.

Although this game can significantly increase your sense of connection with your friends with experience, many individuals initially find it unsettling.

The Guessing Game

(Instructions for Parents/Teachers)

"The Guessing Game" is a very entertaining game that helps improve communication abilities. This game is undoubtedly familiar to you because it is similar to the popular "Twenty Questions" game.

- Start by dividing the group into two groups of nearly similar (or equal) size.
- Ask each team member to leave the room for a minute, then return with an item typically found nearby.
- When the individuals come back, their teammates will ask just "Yes or No" questions (i.e., inquiries that can only be replied with "yes" or "no") to determine what the object is.
- Remind the team that they are competing with the other team and can ask as many inquiries as they need to figure it out.
- Multiple rounds can be used if time permits to increase team competition.

Spend the final ten or so minutes talking and reflecting. Use the following guidelines and inquiries to help it:

Inform the group that it certainly took a lot of time and effort to identify the item every round, but what if we ran out of time and had just one question to ask to identify it?

Closed questions can be highly helpful in some situations to confirm your comprehension or to help you dominate the conversation with an excessively talkative individual or student. Still, open-ended questions are a wonderful way to save time and effort and help you quickly get the information you need.

End of the Word—Beginning of the Next Game

(Instructions for Parents/Teachers)

This is a fun game that keeps your kids involved in honing their listening skills.

The rules are as follows:

The game begins with one person (often an adult) stating one word; it can be any word, but it must be one that every family member can spell.

Following the preceding family member's term, the subsequent member of the group must think of a word that begins with the letter that follows the word.

For instance, the game might cycle through the following list of words:

- Horse
- Ear
- Rest
- Tea

Since you only need a few minutes and the sense of hearing one another, playing this game is simple. This makes it an excellent game to play when in a car, dining room, or long line. By restricting the words to a specific category, such as animals or cities, you can add some complexity to make it more difficult.

Silent Snack Activity

(Instructions for Parents/Teachers)

Finally, "Silent Snack," another activity, allows teens to have fun while honing their interpersonal communication skills.

To attempt it, stick to the following guidelines:

- Set out many different snacks in separate bowls.
- Declare that there will be no chatting during "Silent Snack Time"!
- Give a sample of each snack to each person.
- Take turns expressing your thoughts on each food. Players can express their ideas using facial expressions or gestures like thumbs up and down.
- It's a straightforward endeavor, but it works!

At your next snack time, give it a try.

CHAPTER 2
BETTER RELATIONSHIPS DEVELOPMENT SKILLS

Hey Parents/Teachers!

The teenage years are a time for emotional and social development. Teenagers are developing their potential to be appropriate and sensitive communicators with others, including friends, family, the adults in their lives, while also learning to notice, evaluate, and control their emotions.

Healthy relationships depend on personal qualities like emotional self-regulation, confidence, compassion, communication, and personal abilities. Youth programs frequently don't overtly emphasize fostering meaningful relationships, but they may have activities that encourage pro-social conduct and effective communication. Building healthy connection skills is emphasized in this chapter.

Your child will develop a stronger capacity for compassion, empathy, and communication due to having healthy, respectful connections as they grow up. Your assistance is essential to helping them learn what constitutes a respectful relationship and how to establish one.

The grownups in a teenager's life have the biggest influence over them. Being a good example by maintaining respectful connections with the friends and family you value is the essential thing you can do. Consider the strategies provided in the chapter and how your teen can use them in their interactions with other adults and kids.

Sharing

(For Parents/Teachers)

Teens must learn how to share because it helps in developing and maintaining friendships, playing together, bargaining, and dealing with other people. They learn about tolerance and fairness via sharing. They discover that we can also acquire some of what we want if we offer a bit to others.

Children must have the chance to study and practice sharing. Here are some suggestions about how to promote sharing in daily life:

- Discuss the benefits of sharing with your kid. You may say, "Everyone gets to have fun when they exchange their things with their friend."
- Point out instances of people sharing. For instance, "Your friend was particularly good at sharing her notebooks. She was so kind to do that."
- Give your child lots of praise and attention whenever you notice them attempting to share or take turns. 'I enjoyed how you let Allie play with your videogame, wonderful sharing'!
- Play cooperative and turn-taking games with your youngster. Say things like, "Now it's my turn to build the tower, then it's your turn," as you walk your youngster through the steps. "You give me the red bricks, and I'll give you the green ones".
- Before your child goes on playdates with other kids, discuss sharing with them. Say, for instance, "You'll need to share some of your games when Georgia comes around. Why don't we ask what she wants to play with?" Before starting preschool or child care, you can also discuss sharing with them.

Most kids start understanding that other individuals have feelings by the time they attend middle school. It may still be difficult for them to share a favorite item or game, but kids are now more willing to share and take turns.

Cooperating

(For Parents/Teachers)

We must explain to our youngsters how following rules and requests benefits everyone if we want their cooperation.

The capacity for cooperation is the capacity to balance one's needs with those of others. Cooperation is frequently associated with kids following adult orders. That is conformity. True collaboration entails a give-and-take that is satisfying to both parties. Children need assistance understanding how our demands and rules benefit everyone if they grow up with a cooperative spirit.

Here are some ways you can encourage your kid to cooperate and get its benefits.

Mention the significance of their contribution. This enables them to acknowledge and cherish their abilities. "You assembled the white socks after choosing them all. I was able to complete the wash more quickly. We now have more time for playing." "You arranged the books on the shelf. Making a decision is now simpler. Do you want me to read it aloud to you?"

Offer advice rather than orders. Suggestions encourage participation. Orders frequently meet with resistance. You should try saying, "You should wear a hat because it's cold out. Do you want assistance getting it on, or do you have to do it yourself?

At bedtime, teeth should be brushed. Ask, "Do you need to do it before or after we read our books?" Naturally, they always opt to do it later but don't raise as many objections, and the rule is still followed. Giving your child options demonstrates respect, and respect fosters cooperation.

Listening

(For Parents/Teachers)

A crucial part of learning is listening. A student's capacity for active listening significantly influences the development of necessary communication skills in and out of the classroom.

Active listening is a crucial "soft skill" like problem-solving, management, and collaboration. It's a skill that can be learned and improved, but mastery requires persistence and time.

Giving the speaker your full attention and attempting to comprehend their message are examples of active listening. Both verbal and nonverbal cues of active listening are displayed. Verbal indicators of active listening include affirmation, recalling, and questioning. Examples of nonverbal cues include smiles, head nods, stance, and avoiding outside distractions.

By practicing active listening, parents, teachers, and other caregivers can model how to do the same. Your youngster will understand the value and significance of active listening by watching you practice it. Additionally, it provides your youngster with a framework for creating personal listening practices.

These five suggestions will help you and your teen both develop active listening skills:

1. **Eye Contact**

Eye contact signifies trustworthiness, warmth, sociability, honesty, confidence, and activity. Keeping your eyes focused can help you concentrate better. This makes it easier for you to comprehend what is being spoken fully.

2. **Avoid Interfering**

Before responding, let the other person finish their thought. Do not rush them, finish their sentences, or interrupt them. Avoid speculating or making assumptions about the direction of another person's thoughts; doing so can hinder good communication.

3. Pose Inquiries

Asking specific questions regarding what is being said is one approach to demonstrate that you are paying attention (and ensure you are hearing it accurately). This offers an explanation, guarantees comprehension, and demonstrates that you are paying attention.

Teens Active Listening Activities

The first step in teaching your child to listen actively is to set an example for them. It is crucial to put these abilities into practice. Try some of these exercises to help your kid's listening skills grow and improve.

Cooking with your kid. To complete the recipe correctly, have your child listen to and follow each step as you read it.

Have discussions with your youngster about their interests. This allows your child to participate in a real discussion while honing their speaking and listening skills.

Play the game of telephone. (Discussed in chapter 1) Have a conversation as a group, with each whispering a line to the one after the other. Up until the last person, each person repeats it to the subsequent one. See how much the two sentences differ by having this person read the sentence aloud.

Play the game "*Spot the Change*." Read a brief story to your child. Then, after some revisions, read it again. Have your child clap or raise their hand each time they hear a change.

Make "*follow the directions*" your own. Give your child brief, straightforward instructions, and then ask them to sketch what they hear.

Being a better listener requires a lot of *focus and perseverance*. Students who regularly employ active listening will improve their communication skills and develop lifelong listening abilities.

Respecting Personal Space

(For Parents/Teachers)

For young children in middle school, developing their understanding of and respect for personal space is a crucial social skill. Children who understand and respect others' personal space do better in social situations and close relations with friends and grownups and stay safer.

When the person they are with respects their personal space, everyone feels more at ease.

When peers invade their personal space, kids get uneasy, irritated, and perhaps enraged. We must educate teenagers on the proper use of personal space, how to recognize when they are encroaching on someone else's space, and what to do if they are.

1. Exemplary Personal Space

A crucial first step in educating pupils to respect and use personal space is setting an example. As we go through our busy days and work to assist our kids, it can be easy to overlook this. Even if another person's personal space differs greatly from ours, we must respect it. Our options are;

- Informing children when we must enter their personal space
- Asking children whether we may enter their private space and explaining the reason for doing so.
- Respecting children's need for privacy by saying things like, "I know you don't like it when I touch you, so instead of a high five, I'm sending you a smile."
- Allowing children to observe and hear you doing this with other children and adults.

2. Promote Self-Defense

Teach kids how to detect when someone is intruding on their personal space and how to stand up for themselves if that happens. In certain circumstances, children may have to;

- Back-Up
- Move away.
- Tell the person to stop touching or backing up.

Using Manners

(For Parents/Teachers)

The challenge of teaching your kids manners is well worth the effort. You may believe that polite children are born rather than raised or that your children will learn how to act politely by seeing people around them. While some children have better manners than others, it's still crucial to teach and nurture these virtues in your teenagers.

A child with good manners will be noticed for all the correct purposes. Your child will gain respect from teachers and other parents by practicing good table manners, saying "good" and "thank you," being courteous and respectful, and acting appropriately—which will also help them feel more independent and confident.

However, it can be a little challenging to teach good manners. When their peers in class or online may not be using proper manners, it can be challenging to persuade a teenager to do so. Direct education, roleplaying the desired actions, and, when necessary, reinforcing your objectives with praise and punishments constitute the perfect strategy.

You must decide the manners you wish to teach your child before you begin. Every family will establish its own set of clear expectations for the behavior it wants from its kids. There are some manners, nevertheless, on which almost everyone can agree. These consist of exercising ordinary decency and respect.

These basic manners include training kids to say "kindly," "thank you," "I'm glad," and "you're grateful," as well as to say hello and use appropriate table manners. They also involve requesting permission before touching others or their property and keeping their possessions neat. Other aspects of polite behavior include using inner voices, remaining composed in stressful situations, and resolving disputes equitably.

Once you've created a list of the manners you wish to inculcate in your child, you can begin teaching them. The important thing is to realize that those good manners are just the actions you want your child to exhibit. It is your responsibility as their parents to establish behavioral norms for your children by teaching them what is right or wrong.

1. Maintain Age-appropriate Expectations

Adjust your expectations based on the age and developmental stage of your child. The fundamental phrases "please," "thank you," and "I'm sorry" are not good places to start for teenagers as they already know these basics.

Focusing on one skill at a time, such as basic table manners, can be beneficial before moving on to others, such as the etiquette needed when dining out. Giving your child too much to learn all at once runs the risk of overwhelming them. Additionally, it's beneficial to regularly assess earlier abilities to make sure your teen continues to utilize them and to teach more sophisticated manners they might be prepared to acquire.

2. Use Gratitude

Your teenager wants to win your favor. The more compliments they receive for utilizing their manners, the more probable they will stick. Praise older children when they put their phones down at the dinner table, introduce you to their new buddy without being asked, or introduce you to a stranger properly.

You can either wait till a private moment or immediately provide reinforcement. Remember that certain children, particularly teenagers and those with social anxiety, may feel ashamed and prefer to receive praise without much fanfare. Even if they didn't get it right, you may still commend them for trying. These abilities can take some time to develop and become second nature. Simply observing that they are making an effort can encourage them.

Developing Positive Relationships

(For Parents/Teachers)

Teenagers, as we all know, flourish when they form healthy, pleasant relationships with others. Quality relationships were found to be among the best indicators of middle school students' well-being. Regarding relevance, relationships took precedence over money, a good neighborhood, and even stress from daily life!

Children's relationships have a permanent effect. Even as adults, having early relationships with kind adults and peers is associated with higher levels of achievement, self-worth, and good mental health.

How then can parents foster the circumstances that will enable these crucial connections?

Recognize that fulfilling partnerships don't just happen. They require intention and practice, like most things!

Continue reading for some easy measures you can take to assist teenagers in developing this important ability and get its lifelong rewards.

1. Model Respect

Respect is distinct from some of the other lessons we impart to kids. Start by asking your kids what they think respect means to them. Mention how you listen to them, consider their sentiments, and maintain your composure under pressure as you try to respect them.

Other suggestions are:

- Make a list of polite actions (kind words, compliments, honesty, and excellent manners) and post it somewhere teenagers can see it.
- Discuss what it means to relate respectfully.
- Explain dysfunctional or disrespectful relationships

2. Exercise Mindful Speaking

The act of pausing before speaking has strength. Positive relationships start to take root when kids pick words that benefit rather than hurt. The "Three Gates" method is easy to develop mindful communication. Three gates (or hurdles) must be crossed before we can speak:

- Is it real?
- Is it beneficial?
- Is it decent?

When we speak, we always have an option as to what to say. We may be sure to choose our words more wisely if we take a moment to reflect. We already know that we ought to be honest. However, it's not the only factor to consider. Before we talk, we can consider whether the other person will find our remarks useful and nice.

Also, keep in mind:

- Can you recall a statement you made that appeared accurate but that you afterward felt was unkind or wrong? (Responses could include spreading rumors, criticizing someone, or telling a friend something hurtful someone else said about them.)
- Examining historical circumstances and how the result might have differed utilizing all three "Three Gates" questions.
- Consider ways the "Three Gates" could promote the development of solid relationships.

Parents can engage in mindful speaking by limiting the number of questions they ask their kids. We may make a difference in whether someone feels supported or threatened by our words (e.g., "I'm so delighted you're home" versus "How was school today?" or "Let's take a deep breath together" versus "Why are you crying?").

3. Disagree Politely

It's important to know how to assert oneself appropriately when there is conflict. Kids can learn to argue in ways that can improve relationships in challenging situations!

Think about these choices:

- Allow kids to witness parental conflicts and how they are resolved (when appropriate)
- When there is conflict, in reality, practice calm dialogue. (I was ready to say something unhelpful or unkind, so I'm taking a long breath now.)
- Make a list of possible responses to conflicts, such as sending an "I" message, walking away, negotiating, or approaching an adult for assistance.

Children might just require the appropriate language to disagree respectfully. Here are some possible sentence openers: "Here's what I think," "I disagree, but I'd like to hear more," or "Here's what I think." Deeper degrees of comprehension and engagement may result in this fashion.

4. Develop Empathy

Positive relationships require empathy since it deepens awareness and connection to others. Empathy can be developed through various activities, while it also comes naturally.

Simple tactics consist of:

- Determine their feelings ("Your hands are clenched and your face is flushed. It appears as though you would be angry").
- Talk about disagreements as a family and encourage everyone to see things from the other person's perspective.

Compliment Circle Activity

(For Parents/Teachers)

One of the favorite activities is compliment circles. This instills respect and kindness in the classroom/home and educate teenagers on how to give and accept compliments. Continue reading to learn how to make your classroom/home a place where people give and receive compliments and act with respect and kindness.

Students can learn how to offer and receive compliments through an exercise called a compliment circle. In a complement circle, each student is supposed to complement one of their classmates while also receiving praise from a different student.

Everyone, such as the instructor, sits in a circular form with their legs extended to begin compliment circles. Follow guidelines that I use for teenagers.

I ask for a volunteer to start when I have circle prepared. This person chooses a classmate, calls out their name so everyone can hear, and then compliments them. The complimented friend responds, "Thank you!" before pulling their legs up to sit applesauce-style. The class will then be aware of who still requires praise. After that, you continue in a circle so that everyone has had a chance to give and receive compliments.

The last phase is to allow the students to start coming up with praises on their own by the fourth or fifth circle, and we keep doing that for the rest of the time. I place some restriction that it can't any longer be about their clothing. Those praises are too simple. I want the children to give their peers some serious thought and think about something they witnessed them doing that was kind, or maybe when they realized they were working particularly hard. I urge them to seek positive things their partners are doing during the week so they have ideas for praise when we have our next compliments circle.

While a round completes with compliments, ask kids to read the phrase in the image below. This phrase creates an entertaining environment for teenagers.

Compliment Chain

For all the nice things people say, I will add another link today. And when the chain and floor do meet, Mrs. Moore will bring us a treat.

My Family

(For Teenagers)

This activity aims to strengthen your relationship with your family. Answer the statements and memorize good moments with your family.

My Family

Members in my family that live with me:

_____   _____

_____   _____

_____   _____

Things my family likes to do for fun:

_____   _____

_____   _____

My Family is different from other families because _____

_____

_____

What I really like about my family is_____

_____

_____

Something I would change about my family is_____

_____

_____

My favorite memory of my family is when _____

_____

_____

My least favorite memory of my family is when _____

_____

_____

Family Relationships

(For Teenagers)

What do you like about your family members? Answer the statements to see your closeness with your family members.

Family Relationships

Favourite memory of one another:

What is one trait that you like about one another

Wish to change anything in one another

One thing that you admire about one another

Anything that I have never shared or told before

Things I am sorry for

Wish to change anything about your relationship

Shared Qualities

(For Teenagers)

Think of your close friend and answer the following.

Relationship Building: Shared Qualities

We would like to visit:
1
2
3

Movies, books, or music we like:
1
2
3

We have fun when we:
1
2
3

As friend, we're good at:
1
2
3

As friend, our weaknesses are:
1
2
3

Unique things we have in common:
1
2
3

Qualities we value in a person
1
2
3

Three goals for our future together:
1
2
3

Relationships: Take Charge

(For Teenagers)

Relationships: Take Charge

You are in charge of giving great advice to others on the following key relationship skills when you are working in smart groups or playing games together:

Cooperation:
Explain what it means to cooperate and 1st three rules that group members / friends need to follow

_____
_____
_____
_____
_____

Communication:
Explain what effective communicative looks like and sounds like among friends and classmates

_____
_____
_____

Conflict Resolution:
Explain what effective conflict resolution looks like and sounds like among friends and classmates

_____
_____
_____
_____

Character Relationship

(For Teenagers)

This is time for you to get creative. Think any two characters and create a story. Describe the story as asked.

Character Relationships

Character 1 _____

Character 2 _____

Describe the relationship between the characters at the beginning of the story.

How did the relationship between the characters change by the end of the story?

Why did the relationship between the characters change?

Healthy Relationship

(For Parents/Teachers)

Children and young people should constantly feel respected, valued, supported, and encouraged because healthy connections are fundamentally good. Additionally, kids should be allowed to make their own decisions regarding their actions and words; they shouldn't be forced or bullied into doing anything.

Healthy relationships greatly impact wellness and reduce stress, among other advantages. Additionally, you might find that your teen's life has more meaning and that they are growing socially.

For promoting healthy relationships in the classroom/home, we have compiled seven tips. Which are:

1. **Discuss Limits**

Boundaries aid in both preventing abuse and assisting in the development of healthy relationships that serve the needs and values of children and young people. Encourage kids to consider their own opinions so they may decide where their boundaries lie. This may refer to their overall likes and dislikes in the early years. Older teenagers could entail a personal reflection exercise regarding their beliefs.

Then you may practice expressing boundaries. Young children should be taught that it's acceptable to decline an invitation to do anything, such as hug a family member or participate in an activity and that you will respect them for doing so. Older kids could act out scenarios where one reacts when the other goes too far. They should tell the other person to stop making fun of them, for instance, and if they don't, they should leave and say they don't want to talk while they're doing that.

2. Consider How You Desire to Be Handled in A Relationship

Children will be more aware of unhealthy relationships that don't fit these characteristics if they can articulate how they want to be treated and their rights in a relationship. With some scaffolding as prompts, kids could write down a list of what they anticipate. For instance, reasonable expectations include being treated properly, being respected and encouraged, having the freedom to say no at any moment (even if they've said yes in the past), and not experiencing violence or abuse. Additionally, you might discuss what to do when someone is being abused or exploited and practice identifying such instances.

3. Dispel Stereotypes

Stereotypes can result in abusive behavior and unhealthy relationship expectations, such as punishing people for acting differently than they are "supposed" to. It's crucial to avoid stereotyping from a young age onward; to do this, welcome individuality, encourage boys and girls to play together, and always dispute gender preconceptions when you hear kids reciting them. Try to educate adolescents about the negative effects of stereotyping and how it may be hurtful and unproductive. Adolescents may be particularly prone to it.

Make it abundantly obvious that anyone, regardless of age, color, sexuality, gender identity, or background, is capable of being in toxic relationships and abusing others. Recognizing this to be true can empower victims to speak up in various circumstances.

To know if your teen understands what healthy relationship is, this simple worksheet can help. Just ask your teen to answer the question given in the circle.

Healthy Relationships

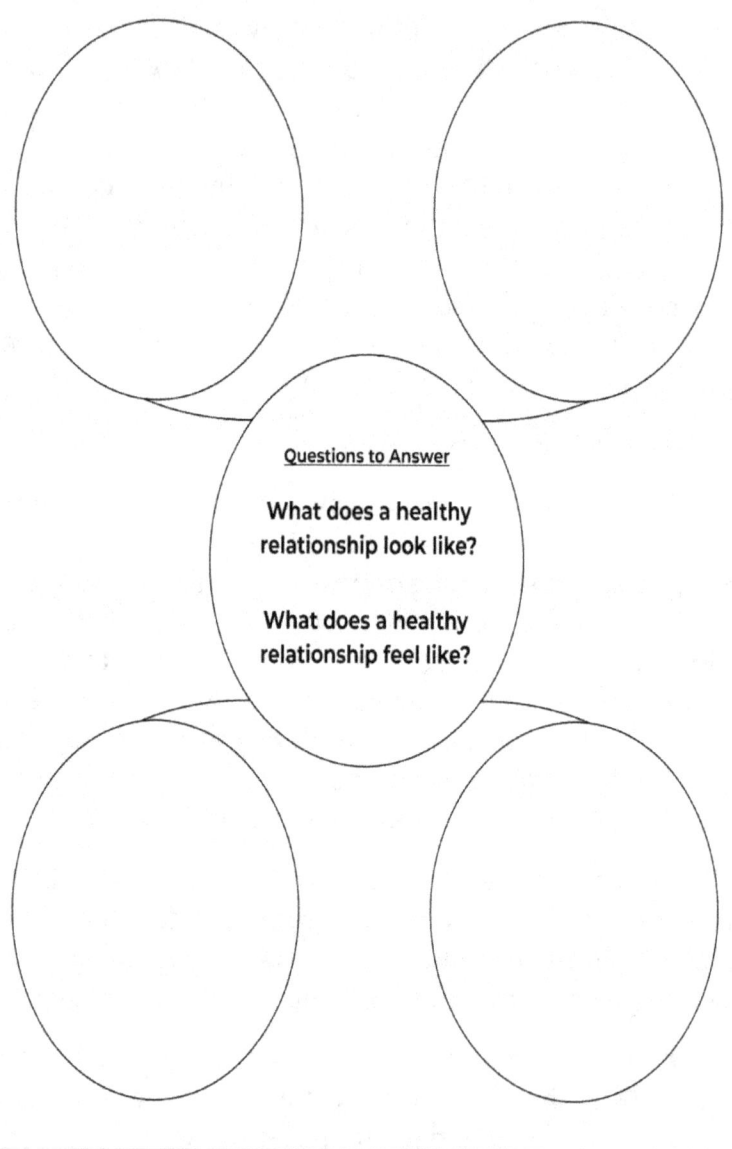

Questions to Answer

What does a healthy relationship look like?

What does a healthy relationship feel like?

Games for Developing Healthy Relationships

(For Teachers/Parents)

Teens/Students' development depends on various relationship skill-building techniques. Here are some developing relationship techniques to follow.

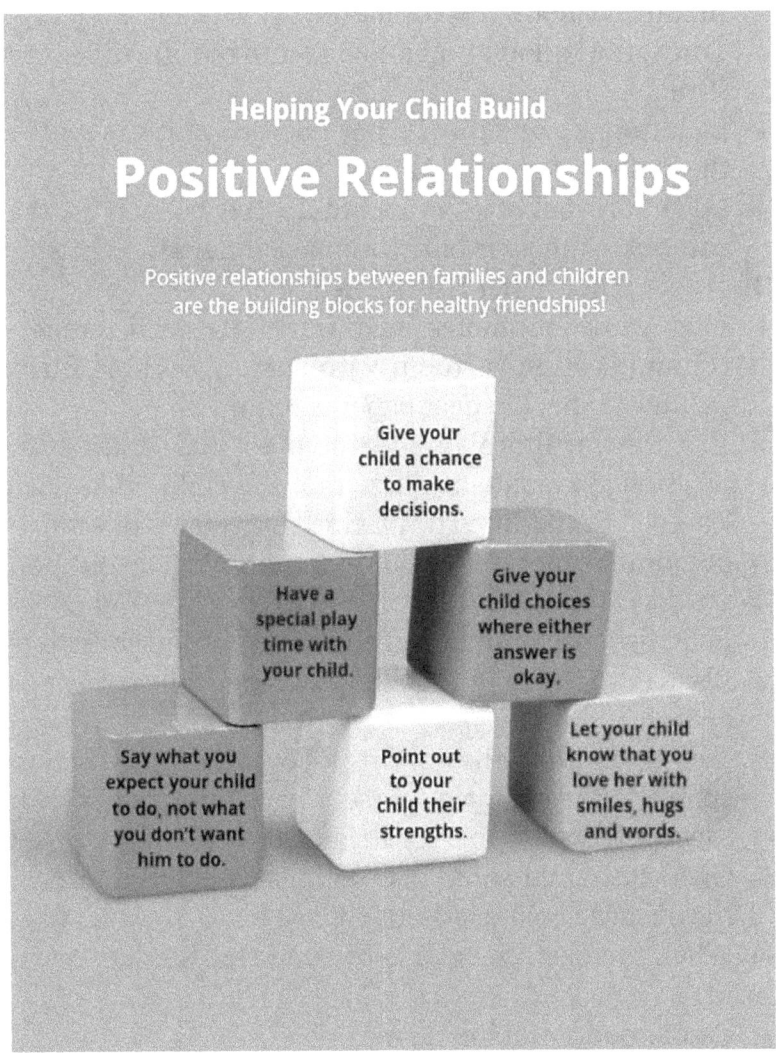

Here are five games you and your kids can play at home that require little to no setup or materials:

1. **Balloon Game**

Playing this game promotes coordination, movement, and teamwork. Multiple family members can be readily included.

- Inflate a balloon (two or more).
- Throw the balloon (or balloons) into the air while standing straight.
- By hitting up and toward one another gently, avoid letting the balloon touch the ground.
- Add more balloons or maintain the balloon in the sky without using your hands to make it harder.

2. **Obstacle Race with Blindfolds**
   - This game promotes teamwork, trust, listening, and communication. A room with some moveable furniture, painter's tape, or sheet paper is required.
   - Use the furniture in the room to pull it into various positions to create a course that the child must navigate. This can be modified by placing large pieces of scrap paper or painter's tape on the floor for the child to avoid stepping on.
   - Establish a beginning and an ending for the child to reach.
   - Place the child at the starting location while covering their eyes.
   - Tell them that they must follow your instructions to complete the obstacle course. They must start over if they touch any tape, paper, or furniture.
   - Give your child some instructions to help them navigate the obstacle course effectively.
   - When the obstacle course becomes too simple, rearrange it.
   - Go blinded by taking turns!

3. Mirroring

This game encourages intense focus, impulsivity, and silliness! There are no setup or supply requirements.

Meet your child face to face.

- The participant has to mirror the calm and straightforward movements made by the leader.
- For a greater challenge, the leader can make moves more complicated.
- Take turns in commanding!

4. Hockey with Cotton Balls

This game promotes deep, controlled breathing while serving as a competition among parents and teens.

- At a clean table, take a seat opposite one another.
- On each side of the table, mark a "goal" using scrap paper or any other tiny object.
- Without using their hands, each player uses a straw to push a cotton ball across the table while attempting to keep it out of their personal goal and into the other player's.
- Play till you are exhausted, or keep scoring!

These games can be played for as long as you like. Playing with your children for a short while can enhance positive interactions in your family and give them the devoted attention, they require from you. Play these games one-on-one with a child who might require extra care with the entire family, or teach your siblings to play them together to promote a better sibling connection.

CHAPTER 3

INCREASING HAPPINESS SKILLS

(For Parents/Teachers)

We all want our children to be happy, wholesome and content

But...

Did you realize that cultivating happiness is a skill?

It is said that happiness is something we can choose and develop rather than something that just comes to us.

A pleasant, healthy childhood could prepare your children for success in adulthood. However, many parents are curious about how to raise content children in the modern environment. Giving your children temporary pleasure or instant gratification won't make them happy. In actuality, the opposite of the sentence is true.

A skill set enables happy children to experience long-term enjoyment in life. They can forgo immediate gratification to accomplish their objectives. By forming wholesome, lifelong habits, you can aid in your children's development of these abilities.

Remember that children don't always need to be joyful all the time. People must also go through unpleasant feelings like despair, rage, anxiety, and disappointment. When your children feel unpleasant, there's no need to encourage them or take action. Instead, offer them support while they go through it and assist them in discovering coping mechanisms for their emotions.

If kids aren't happy all the time, it doesn't speak poorly of your parenting. The happiness of your children is not your responsibility. Instead, it's your responsibility to teach your kids how to control their emotions in healthy ways. Giving children a caring environment is the greatest thing you can do to produce happy children. Even amid challenging circumstances, children who feel loved and cared for are more likely to thrive. Thus, the aim of this chapter is to help you and your teenager to have a happy and fulfilling life. The strategies, activities and games have been designed specially to make your teen's life full of gratitude and happiness.

Playing Outside and Practice Positivity

(For Parents/Teachers)

Never undervalue the influence of outdoor play. Children benefit from playing outside, climbing trees, swinging, and digging in the soil. According to studies, natural aromas like lavender, cut grass, and pine trees help improve your child's happiness.

To help your child feel happier immediately, you might urge them to read a book or do their work on the porch. Playing outside can help kids' social skills. Children who spend more time playing outside develop important social skills, including empathy, involvement, and self-control.

According to one study, youngsters with higher social abilities are twice as likely to attend college and are less likely to engage in violent behavior, abuse drugs, or be obese. So, make playing outside a daily ritual. Urge your youngsters to ride their bikes, play with other kids in the area, and run around in the big outdoors even when the weather isn't ideal. Happiness requires practice, like training to throw the ball or play the piano. Every day, dedicate a brief period to thinking positively. Spend some time reflecting on the positive aspects of the day before bed or during a meal.

Train Your Brain

(For Parents/Teachers)

Teach your children to look around them for the things they appreciate, which bring them joy. Teach children to look for the things and people they like in a new environment. Many parents might not fully understand brain training for children or its purpose.

So, what is it exactly?

Mindfulness conditioning is a process that requires knowledge, learning, and perception of things to strengthen neural connections for simple understanding. Concentration enhancement, memory consolidation, and increased intellectual flexibility are the three most obvious benefits of brain training.

Why is it vital to train children's brains?

The need for mental health in every child is a straightforward response. Children can fully develop if parents look after their physical and emotional needs. Children who receive brain training from a young age will also be more likely to have the proper perspective and awareness of their surroundings.

Because of this, do not disregard your children's need for cognitive practice. Remember the next three parenting pieces of advice to help your kids' mental health.

1. Encourage Personalized, Active Learning

This is yet another vital piece of advice for your cognitive training. Rather than trying to cram information into your children, encourage their curiosity! You can enhance their learning by bringing kids on outings to a park, zoo, museum, or library. You can start conversations with your kids about any subject to get them thinking, asking questions, and expressing their thoughts. Allow them to pursue new interests like playing a musical instrument if they choose. The goal of the brain training method has been accomplished as long as your children are happy, excited, and eager to learn.

2. Plays for the Brain

We are all aware that youngsters can experience discouragement due to too much knowledge. Then is when you should engage in some enjoyable activities. Don't assume that giving your kids video games will spoil them. On the other hand, playing in a regulated and controlled manner will benefit them. Children must pay close attention while playing games and rhythmically coordinate their hands, feet, ears, and vision for reflexes. Given that the brain must function at its highest level, this undoubtedly increases the effectiveness of cognitive training for children.

3. Be A Companion, A Friend, and A Guide.

Last but not least, but most crucially, attempt to be a friend, a companion, and a leader. The parents' contribution is crucial in assisting children with a completely formed brain training process. Parents stick by their children from a young age, watching them develop into adults who can support themselves. The way parents raise their children has a big impact on the child's development. As a result, you participate in cognitive training as well.

And here's some advice for you: Communicate, empathize, and offer assistance whenever possible. That does not imply that you will be kind to the kids. Be firm when they misbehave, encouraging when they falter, and joyful when they achieve.

However, you have to be friends. Let's listen to their stories and experiences while sharing your thoughts, feelings, and experiences with them. Your children will be able to develop their emotional intelligence in this way as well. You can be a dependable friend who experiences all the highs and lows of life and is always there for them. Along with helping your children define themselves, you can also serve as a guide, demonstrating many facets of life to them. In other words, the effectiveness of your children's brain activities depends largely on you.

Install Happiness Triggers

(For Parents/Teachers)

This is a fantastic concept for a kid's room and a method to change how you view your entire home. Happiness is increased when unique items and memories are conspicuously displayed, such as a letter from a grandparent, pictures of friends, or a souvenir from a memorable occasion.

One of the best ways to encourage youngsters to form genuinely beneficial social bonds is by teaching them how to spread happiness. We teach kids how to be supportive and inclusive, write letters to one another, and communicate with elderly relatives. We emphasize friendship and challenge them to consider how they may be better friends. Giving praises, expressing gratitude, and helping others are all part of spreading happiness.

Children will realize that it is always within their power to shift their attitude for the better once they realize their brain reacts/lights up in the same way of giving and receiving things.

Write it Down

(For Teenagers)

Strong psychological advantages of writing include enjoyment, creativity, and assistance creating the life we want. Numerous writing activities, including creative writing, expressive journaling, and goal-setting, have been linked to happiness. Discover the top ways that writing can make your life happy.

1. **Writing helps people feel better and process their feelings.**

The benefits of writing for the sole purpose of getting your thoughts onto paper are enormous for mental health. A recent study looked at 81 undergraduate students to see how writing affected them. For five months, the kids wrote for 20 minutes daily about real-life issues like traumatic experiences and aspirations. By the time the project was finished, it had significantly increased participants' well-being and mood.

Why?

Writing provides a safe space to express worries and fears. Increased happiness and decreased stress are two therapeutic benefits of writing thoughts down on paper or in a notebook. In light of this, make an effort to use journaling to communicate and process life events to help you move forward in a constructive manner.

2. **Writing helps us see ourselves more objectively.**

There isn't a better method to understand your cognitive processes than to put them in writing. Writing down feelings shows mental patterns that lead to new insights about the causes of those feelings in the first place.

Past events may trigger our automatic defensive mechanism, and emotions may arise to defend us without our awareness or understanding. For instance, a person who recently experienced a terrible breakup can exhibit timidity, avoid getting near strangers and isolate themselves. Writing helps us realize how our emotions are rooted in the past, allowing us to heal rather than preventing us from fully experiencing life gradually.

Practice Gratitude

(For Parents/Teachers)

You can influence children's happiness and health by incorporating thankfulness into daily life. But remember that there's a great difference between saying "thank you" merely to say it and mean it.

As per a 2013 study on gratitude, those who practice it have firm connections, which can be essential to a happier existence. Modeling gratitude is one of the finest methods to encourage kids to feel true gratitude.

Have High but Achievable Expectations

(For Parents/Teachers)

Children who attempt to do difficult things are likely to have fulfilled lives, even though spending hours preparing for a test or practicing an instrument is not enjoyable. Your aspirations significantly influence how willing your youngster is to take on new challenges. When your standards are reasonable, your children will try to understand them.

Studies have shown that children do well in class and stick longer at challenging activities. High standards are associated with social and academic resilience.

However, it's crucial to remember that you shouldn't anticipate perfection. It's likely to backfire if you set your child's expectations too high. Your child will likely experience mental health issues if you want them to be perfect. When child thinks that you've set the expectations very high, she might give up on the objectives you've set for her.

Teach Self-Control

(For Parents/Teachers)

Kids may experience brief pleasure from eating an extra chocolate, and watching TV longer than usual rather than finishing their responsibilities.

Begin instilling self-discipline in your child. Teach her not to be tempted by too many things simultaneously. You could help her in achieving this in several ways, such as the following:

- Place a basket for cell phones in the kitchen area. To prevent her from being tempted to browse the internet while doing her homework, advise your child to place her cellphone in the basket while she is working on it.
- Before going to bed, place all electronics in a shared room.
- Stock up on nutritious food options in the kitchen.

Freeze Dance

Before Beginning

Select a place that is open and unimpeded. Point out immovable items and caution everyone not to touch them or any other people or objects by doing so. Select the proper station or music on the music player or radio.

BEST FOR

| Any number of kids | Pre-K to 3rd Grade | Under 10 minute teaching time | No equipment needed | Virtual play |

HOW TO PLAY

The goal of the game is to **freeze instantly when the music stops playing.** The leader plays music and players dance.

When the **music stops, each player must freeze immediately** and hold that position until the music begins again.

If a player does **not freeze immediately,** they must **complete five jumping jacks** and can then rejoin the dancing.

Time for jumping jacks!

5x

Therapy Games for Teens & Middle School

Things that make me Happy Activity

(For Teens)

The Feeling of the Day Activity

(For Teens)

FEELING OF THE DAY: "HAPPY"

Happy means: **feeling good, feeling satisfied, or having a good time.**

What does being happy mean to me?

When do I feel happy?

When I am Feeling Happy Worksheet
(For Teens)

When I'm Feeling....  HAPPY

This is me, when I am feeling happy

When I feel happy. I might also feel

All emotions are ok, but not all behaviors are ok

When I am feeling happy, I like to do those things.

- _____
- _____
- _____

Happy and Mad

(For Teens)

I feel happy when _____

You can tell when I'm happy because my face _____

I can tell when other people are happy because they _____

I get mad when _____

You can tell when I'm mad because my face _____

I can tell when other people are mad because they _____

When I'm mad. I know I should _____

Happy Words

(For Teens)

Write down some words or sentences that make you happy.

My Happy Sheet

(For Teens)

My Happy Sheet

Use this worksheet to write or draw things that make you happy and bring a smile to your face. Keep this sheet somewhere close by when you feel yourself setting upset, anxious or scared, pull this sheet out to help you cope with those feelings

My Feel Happier Flower

(For Teens)

Write down about the things that make you happy in flower petals. Write things that make you feel unhappy in rain drops. Color them.

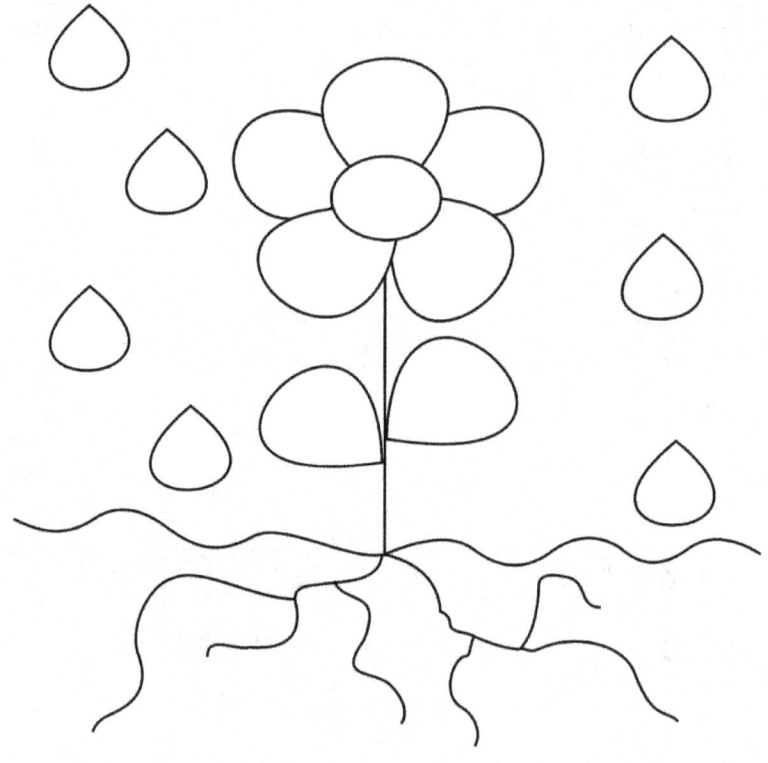

CHAPTER 4
GREATER EFFICIENCY & CREATIVITY SKILLS

(For Parents/Teachers)

Creativity skills boost your children's inventive abilities and advance their thought processes. It gives kids the ability to think creatively at a young age. Modern education mandates instructional methods that standardize evaluation, motivating kids to create and innovate. It motivates students with the standards of fundamental knowledge. Give your kids the freedom to imagine how they want the real world to be. They can then understand the concreteness of competence in this way.

The Importance of Creativity

Parental involvement in creative learning is significant and productive. It is vital for its function and essential. Learning begins for children in the cradle. Parents thus serve as their children's first teachers. They are also the first facilitators and leaders. Parents have a significant impact on their children's learning and creativity.

The vast edifice of education is built on the foundation of creative learning. Children's minds begin to grow through learning, where they are the "blank slates." Creative activities heavily influence the standards of childhood education. We must all make an effort to create a field of education that will survive forever through creative learning.

Children with creative abilities have better capacities and are more aware of the solutions to challenges that arise in the actual world. The imagination and intuition are strengthened and enhanced via activity-based learning.

When parents support their children's curiosity, their ability to think creatively increases. They can encourage inventive thinking by drawing on everyday activities. This gives the kids confidence and sparks fresh ideas. Parents and teachers have a part to play in fostering creative learning in children. They must take on a facilitative or guiding role. They should help and educate the kids as they introduce innovations, which are the foundation of creative thinking.

It makes learning more effective. Doing so can ensure that our children's learning is successful and oriented deeply. Children's bright futures can be shaped with the aid of creative thinking. This chapter will be focusing on creativity skills of teenagers.

(The following strategies are for Parents/Teachers)

First Things First

Teach students how to prioritize tasks for tests and exams. For instance, before tackling more challenging questions, answer all the questions for which you already have the answer. Kids needs assistance creating very succinct summaries in answer to different queries. Reduce distractions and increase efficiency by sitting at the front of the classroom, having all things ready and available when the test is handed out, and using a watch as a timer to track how much time is left on the test.

Break It Down

Ask youngsters to break down their big tasks. For instance, reduce the size of larger assignments. You can ask your kid to manage time spent on chores by breaking major projects into smaller ones that can be finished at specific times and days. Split the weekly projects into monthly and specify that specific project components must be completed by the end of each week for a youngster whose science fair project is due in a month.

Time Tracking

Post a big, household monthly calendar in the center of the house, along with smaller schedules all over the place. On the huge monthly family calendar, arrange and rank the daily commitments, activities, and events using different colored markers. For hectic weeks or weekends, use the shorter schedules. Insist on using the time between appointments to take care of chores around the house. Encourage the youngster to prioritize tasks like finishing homework, playing with friends, performing housework, and going to extracurricular activities like this.

Watch for Weariness

Keep an eye out for persistent under-arousal in children since it could indicate a slow cognitive pace. Keep an eye on her to determine if she simply takes things very slowly or sluggishly or if she appears bored with everything. This can indicate an inattentive type of ADHD or a generally slow cognitive pace. If this continues, talk to her pediatrician about possible medical or dietary problems.

Encourage

The educational experience of your child extends outside the boundaries of the classroom. Children naturally possess intuition and spontaneity, so encouraging these qualities in them will undoubtedly increase their creativity. You merely need to instruct them to act on their original ideas and quick wit; there is no need to plan everything carefully. It will further promote spontaneity and the capacity for self-expression. Make them more adaptable so they may employ their innate intelligence more frequently, a requirement for creativity.

Give Them a Space

Give your child lots of room to construct, sketch, or create whatever they desire. Along with helping kids become more creative, it improves their memory, problem-solving abilities, and cognitive capabilities. Ask your kid, "what else could this be used for?" to encourage them to be an inventor. To help them develop their imagination, challenge them to use unusual techniques to produce something. You could also give them building blocks and ask them to build some surprising characters from them, or you could ask them to design and produce the birthday candy labels themselves.

Self-Reliance

Children need to learn to trust in their potential and ability and be assured of the truth of their thoughts. Then, it becomes imperative for you to refrain from interfering with others' abilities to make decisions. Encourage your child to speak up for what they believe, feel, or think as long as it is inherent since self-reliance is a rare attribute that opens the door to accomplishing anything significant in life. For your child to think that they can affect change in the world, creativity necessitates that their choice comes first above all else.

Participate in Healthy Competition

Competition brings out the best in people. It also applies to children, but you shouldn't push them to succeed because it could have the opposite effect on them. Inform them that it is not important to rank first or last or to do better than others. It merely involves bringing out their full potential and making them aware of their capabilities. Therefore, healthy competition ensures that your child won't feel pressured to perform well all the time and will instead feel free to express himself, create, and dream. Encourage children to participate in sports, the arts, music, plays, or theatre. As a result, they will begin to believe in their creativity, enabling them to realize their aspirations.

Encourage Confidence

One of the most crucial conditions for fostering creativity in your child is confidence. Every area of their lives is impacted by it. Kids won't significantly advance until they have adequate confidence in their skills and interests. Give your child the opportunity to experience being adventurous by taking them for hiking, running, leaping, skating, or exploring the outdoors. Utilize various circumstances to encourage your child's imagination and feeling of adventure.

Creative Drawing

(For Teens)

There are 9 boxes in the image with different shapes. Can you draw something using these shapes?

Beach Story

(For Teens)

Create a story by looking at the characters in the image.

Creative Writing Sheet

(For Teens)

It is a fun activity. There is a situation given in the picture. Can you tell me a scenario that you think of after reading the situation?

If Christopher Columbus discovered the America in 2492, he would have found.....

Imagining Pet Creativity

(For Teens)

Now try this situation.

Creative Writing

What if you had a dinosaur as a pet? What would you feed it? Where would you keep it? Don't forget dinosaurs have names too?

Time Machine Fun Activity

(For Teens)

Share your thoughts in the worksheet below.

Time Machine

If you had a time machine, where would you go and what would you do? Who would you talk to? (150 words)

If I had a time machine, I would...

Games to Develop Creativity Skills

(For Parents/Teachers)

Every child's creative, cognitive, and social development depends on the play. Here are some simple games you may play with children.

1. Wander through Wonderland

Take your kids for a stroll in the sunshine and engage them in conversation by asking them open-ended questions as you go. Some instances include:

- What do you suppose the dog in the garden is looking for?
- What do you suppose our next-door neighbor Mrs. Jane enjoys doing on a Saturday night?
- Where do you suppose fairies and elves would be hiding if they lived in our neighborhood?
- What color would you choose to paint that house if you had the option?

Encourage your children to make intriguing observations for you as well. They will always have distinct and frequently unexpected viewpoints to give on a variety of subjects. They will always amaze you with their vivid imaginations because the universe is so new and intriguing to them!

2. Prepare a Feast

Getting your kids involved in home cooking is a good way to inspire them to express their creativity. You might help them bake a cake and ask them to design it, or you could come up with a novel and unusual recipe you can both try out.

Once their dish has been prepared, ask them whom they would like to share it with. Do they want a friend to visit? Grandma and Grandpa, or even the family cat, might join in. Let them make that decision. Your youngster will have the opportunity to think more freely about their house and the wider world by using common objects in new ways.

3. Get Musical

You don't need to invest in pricey musical equipment to establish a band and unleash the budding rock stars in your children. After taking them out of the cabinet, set out a few pots, pans, and wooden spoons in the living room. Then play your children's favorite music so they can participate.

Allow them to generate noise without forcing them to adhere to certain styles, structures, or melodies. While kids develop creative new drum beats, they'll like watching you dance along, and the action will improve their gross motor abilities.

4. Hold a Costume Contest

Give your kids opportunity to dress up in bizarre, eye-catching attire by allowing them access to your closet, old jumble bags, and dress-up costume chest. Give them a topic to work with or leave it up to their imaginations.

The most crucial thing in this situation is for you to let down your guard and demonstrate to your children how much you cherish their creativity and imagination. They'll have more fun and come up with fantastic ideas for your upcoming family costume party the more you engage them in decision making.

5. Play 'What If?'

What If? is an easy game that can be played anywhere and is a great way to test your kids' inventiveness, even though it can occasionally become goofy. You have to come up with amusing circumstances that will force them to use their creative thinking to devise innovative solutions.

Query them on things like;

- What would happen if giraffes could reach the moon in height?
- How about the ability to travel anywhere by car?
- Suppose you were ten feet tall.
- What if there was perpetual sunshine and the sun never set?
- "What if cows bleated and horses meowed?"

and so forth. Your kids will have more fun answering more bizarre questions!

6. Colors and Names

This is another simple game that you can enjoy anywhere in a store, on the bus, or while unwinding with the kids at home. To begin, have your kids list as many objects as possible that are a specific color, such as yellow.

Next, ask them how many objects they can name that have an oval form, how many items they can conceive that begin with the letter "L," and so on. Create competition by continuing the game with new examples and keeping scores. To encourage children to think beyond the box, you could even give small rewards for the most imaginative responses.

PART-II

SKILLS FOR BUILDING SELF-ESTEEM

Hey Teenagers!

The ability to be confident is a state of mind; it cannot be learned like a set of rules. Thinking positively, exercising, learning, gaining knowledge, and conversing with others are all effective ways to build or increase your confidence.

Feelings of wellbeing, tolerance of your mind and body (your self-esteem), and faith in your capability, abilities, and experience are the sources of confidence. The majority of people wish they were more confident. Though, it can mean things to different people, having self-confidence just means believing in yourself.

Our upbringing and education have a lot to play in how confident we are. We pick up our behavior and way of thinking from other people, and these teachings impact how we see ourselves and others. Our experiences and how we've honed our responses to various circumstances affect how confident we feel.

Self-confidence is a dynamic indicator. Our confidence level in our ability to carry out duties and activities and handle situations might fluctuate, and sometimes we may feel much more confident than others. Willing to trust your judgment, capabilities, and abilities is a sign of self-confidence. We feel more self-sufficient when we see ourselves attaining our goals and learning new talents. Thus, this part is dedicated to some skills that help you in boosting your self-esteem. Keep reading to boost your self-confidence.

CHAPTER 5
CHALLENGING NEGATIVE BELIEFS

(For Teens)

Feeling gloomy is normal if your mind is racing with bad ideas. You can take steps to improve the situation, even if it won't be simple to tune out the bad sounds. The difficulty with self-talk is that it still feels true, even when it's biased or untrue. Self-talk is your internal monologue. You probably have downward spiraling self-talk if you have negative ideas.

It could take time and practice to become adept at challenging this mood, but the effort is worthwhile. You'll be startled to realize how much of your thinking is directed toward a pessimistic view of things once you start tracking how frequently you hear the negativity.

Automatically pessimistic ideas influence emotions and negatively skew our picture of reality. Because they are temporary and repetitive, these ideas are challenging to identify. We can get angry, anxious, less productive, impair our relationships, or experience psychological injury due to negative thinking.

By confronting and rephrasing the negative habitual thoughts positively, it is possible to overcome these behaviors easily. We all experience negative thoughts occasionally, but if you feel you can't get out of your slump, it's critical to know that you can overcome your self-doubt. Developing the skill of confronting your conversation will pay off greatly because no unpleasant path is ever permanent. This chapter will focus on developing skills that will help you to challenge negative belief.

Understand Your Thought Patterns

(For Teens)

The identification of negative automatic thought patterns is beneficial exercise to try. We occasionally view unpleasant or upsetting circumstances similarly without considering the supporting data. We might engage in a wide range of negative thought processes. Typical examples include:

- Thinking in black and white, where everything is either one way or another, and there is no grey area.
- *Personalizing*: When we think we are to blame for everything that goes wrong, we fail to consider other potential causes.
- Filter thinking is the tendency to focus on the negative aspects of situations.
- Catastrophizing is assuming the worst-case scenario will occur.

When we identify these harmful thought patterns, we can swap them out for more constructive ones.

1. Common Forms of Negative Thoughts

Thinking at All or Nothing: You only see things in terms of black and white. You view yourself as a complete failure if your performance isn't flawless.

Overgeneralization: You interpret a single unfavorable experience as a recurring pattern of failure.

Mental filter: You focus solely on one negative aspect of reality, allowing the rest of reality to fade into the background like an ink drop tainting a whole beaker of water.

Disqualifying the good is claiming that happy experiences "don't count" for whatever reason. You can do this to continue holding a false belief at odds with your life's reality.

Jumping to Conclusions: You draw a negative conclusion without concrete evidence supporting it.

Mind Reading: Without further research, you arbitrarily assume someone is responding badly to you.

Telling Your Fate: You believe that things will not work out well and are adamant that your forecast has already come to pass.

Emotional Reasoning: You believe that since you feel something, it must be true. This is known as the "I feel it. Therefore, it must be true" fallacy.

Should Statements: Should statements make you feel angry, frustrated, and resentful toward the other person.

You mistakenly believe that you were mostly responsible for some terrible external incident, despite the reality that you were not.

Start a Thought Diary

(For Parents/Teachers)

Keeping a thought journal is another approach to halt bad thoughts. With the help of this tool, we may recognize our destructive thought patterns and improve our comprehension of how our thoughts might influence our emotional responses.

A teen's life might gradually change by altering the thought pattern and substituting it with ideas focused on a certain therapeutic goal. A teen might be instructed to keep a thought journal to accomplish this. It's a tool to track emotions, including fear, hurt, rage, guilt, humiliation, and melancholy. An adolescent would record these experiences, the times and locations, and any accompanying thoughts they had at the time.

Finding harmful and self-defeating beliefs might be easier by reflecting on one's self-talk in a particular setting. That's not all, though. A thinking journal also encourages a teen to record a different idea that is more beneficial, realistic, and encouraging.

The new mindset can be "I can do this," for instance, rather than "I am useless." Teens undergoing therapy would discover that constructive ideas encourage self-acceptance. Additionally, they express preferences instead of ideas that make unwavering demands using terms like "should" or "must."

Then adolescents are encouraged to use their new, alternate thoughts, especially in comparable situations. The process of differentiating feelings continues throughout therapy. Other emotions like irritation, worry, regret, or remorse are also investigated to understand how different emotions affect a teen's behaviors and decisions.

A teenager's awareness of feelings, ideas, and behaviors is further increased by using the thought diary to score the intensity of emotions. The capacity to become more mindful helps people make conscious decisions instead of snap judgments that undermine their self-worth. This is a crucial factor for an adolescent to succeed.

Ability-Talk, Effort-Talk, Self-Talk

(For Teens)

The method of redefining your negative self-talk to produce a positive shift in your mentality is known as challenging negative beliefs. However, it does require a little more work than simply attempting to think optimistically. To begin with, it's beneficial to weigh your work versus the result.

Children who used positive "effort-talk" performed better in mathematics than those who used positive "self-talk," "ability-talk," or no self-talk at all. According to the study, the differences are as follows:

"I am good at this!" is the ability-talk.

Effort-talk: "I'll give it my all."

Self-talk, "I'll succeed!"

Positive effort-talkers could free themselves from any doubts they may have had about their skills and talents by putting effort before results.

Cultivate Self Awareness

(For Teens)

The tendency to talk negatively to ourselves is frequently instinctive since the mind is wired to focus on the bad. So, becoming aware that you have negative ideas is the first step toward addressing them.

It's important to be conscious of both the words and the context in which you use them. You can build the self-awareness required to question your negative ideas by becoming aware of the triggers, what you're saying, and why you're saying it.

There are numerous methods to develop and exercise self-awareness; however, the following are some of the most successful ones:

1. Start Meditating and Practicing Mindfulness

Being mindful is focusing on the present and being aware of the surroundings instead of getting caught up in thought, meditating, or daydreaming. The act of spending time on one thing during meditation such as your breathing, a mantra, or a feeling while allowing your ideas to pass by without holding on to them will help to be self-aware. Engaging in either exercise can improve your awareness of your internal representation and responses to situations. Additionally, they can assist you in recognizing your emotions and thoughts so that you don't lose sight of who you are by being overcome by them.

2. Engage in Yoga

Although yoga is a physical exercise, it is also a cerebral exercise. Your mind develops self-control, self-acceptance, and awareness as your body stretches, bends, and flexes. You become more conscious of both your body and all the feelings it experiences and your mind and thoughts that run through it. Yoga can even be combined with mindfulness practices like meditation to increase self-awareness.

3. Set Aside Time to Think.

The key to effective reflection is to examine your thoughts, feelings, and behaviors to determine where you fulfilled your standards, where you fell short of them, and where you may do better. This can be done in various methods, including journaling (already discussed in detail).

Practice Self-Love

(For Teens)

Self-love is a feeling of admiration for oneself that develops through behaviors that promote our mental, emotional, and spiritual development. Having a high respect for your happiness and well-being is what it means to love yourself. Self-love entails attending to your requirements and refraining from putting your health at risk to please others. Not settling for much less than you deserve is a sign of self-love.

Since we all have a variety of ways to care for ourselves, self-love can mean different things to different people. Your mental wellness depends on finding out what self-love means to you personally. How to practice loving yourself includes:

Being Conscious. People who value themselves are more likely to be aware of their thoughts, feelings, and desires.

Taking Good Care of Oneself. When you better meet your needs, you will love yourself more. People with a high level of self-love take care of themselves daily by engaging in healthy habits, including good eating, exercise, rest, intimacy, and constructive social connections.

Finally, to practice self-love, start treating yourself with the same compassion, kindness, and care you would show to a loved one. Another important factor in eliminating negative thoughts is compassion for oneself. We need to fully accept who we are, our faults, and accept the truth that we are flawed.

Dispute the Irrational Thoughts

(For Teens)

It can be beneficial to consider any data that contradicts the unfavorable ideas you're feeling. If you believe, for example, that you are bad at your work, consider whether there is any proof to the contrary. Has your teacher or parent recently given you an appreciation for your work? You can boost your self-confidence and reaffirm your ability by refuting the thought with supportive evidence.

The exercise requires you to look for supporting data. Finding an occurrence that supports your belief is necessary for evidence. You can only think or believe that something is awful. Grab a blank piece of paper and write your irrational belief at the top to begin the debating exercise. Make sure to say it out loud and clearly.

Next, ask yourself, "Is there any proof that my belief is accurate?" Then, type your response. Then, ask yourself, "What horrible could happen to me if I maintain that belief?" Then, type your response. Write "**What Good Can Happen to Me If I Keep My Belief**?" as your final sentence.

Ways to Challenge Negative Thoughts

(For Teens)

Here are some ways to challenge your negative thoughts.

WAYS TO CHALLENGE NEGATIVE THOUGHTS

- AM I JUMPING TO NEGATIVE CONCLUSIONS?
- WHAT IS A MORE HELPFUL THOUGHT?
- WHAT CAN I DO THAT WILL HELP ME SOLVE THE PROBLEM?
- WHAT WOULD I SAY TO A FRIEND?
- WILL THIS MATTER IN A FEW MONTHS OR YEARS?
- WHAT ARE OTHER POSSIBLE OUTCOMES?
- WHAT WOULD BE ANOTHER WAY TO LOCK AT IT?

All or Nothing Thinking

(For Teens)

Think of a situation that happens with you and answer the following.

How to Crush
ALL-OR-NOTHING THINKING

Describe the situation.

(Current) Thoughts, Emotions, Actions	(New) Thoughts, Emotions, Actions
Capture the stories you tell.	What thoughts would create the new emotions?
Pinpoint the emotions your story triggers.	What emotion would drive the desired action?
Describe the result of your thoughts and emotions.	What is your desired action?

Overcoming Negative Thoughts

(For Teens)

Overcoming Negative Thoughts

A common negative thought I have is:

Questions to ask myself:

Is this thought true?

Do I have supporting evidence that this is true?

What's the worst that could happen?

What's the best that could happen?

Am I having this thought because I'm unhappy about something else?

Am I blaming someone else without taking responsibility?

Am I jumping to conclusions?

Automatic Negative Thoughts

(For Teens)

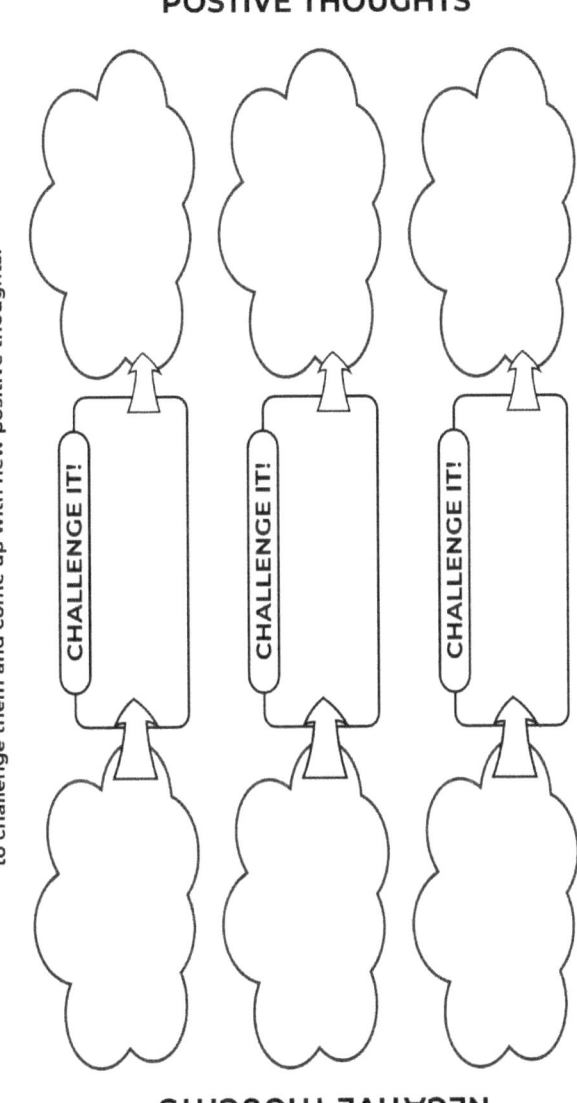

Therapy Games for Teens & Middle School

Changing Negative Thoughts

(For Teens)

Negative Thoughts

It is John's first day at his new school. He is having negative thoughts that are making him feel anxious. Can you help him change his thoughts?

- I don't have any friends here. No one is going to like me!
- My friends at my old school are having fun without me.
- I'm so nervous! The kids will probably think that I'm weird.
- This school is SO big. I know for sure that I'm going to get lost!

Challenging Negative Thoughts

(For Teens)

Challenging Negative Thoughts

Change your thoughts. change your reality.

What am I upset/worried about?

How are my emotions affecting my behavior?

How are my beliefs/expectations irrational in this situation?

What is a more positive and realistic way of viewing this situation?

Gratitude

(For Teens)

Consider a time when you expressed gratitude to someone for their assistance, encouragement, or even their presence in your life.

How did you and that person feel at that time?

Perhaps you can recall when someone offered you something to symbolize their appreciation—not something you requested or purchased. Didn't it feel fairly good?

There are countless methods to express thanks to people, to oneself, to a higher force, or even to "the universe." However, without useful tips, it may be difficult to begin. These gratitude exercises and activities are some of the most well-known and effective ways to practice and improve your thankfulness.

1. Positivity Rocks

This exercise might seem a bit absurd. You may be asking yourself, "A rock? How might a rock assist me in developing gratitude? The rock is a symbol and a tangible object you can use to remind yourself of what you have, which is the trick to this activity. Just finding a rock is all that is required to follow the directions.

- Choose one that you enjoy, whether it is because it is attractive, smooth, or has an intriguing texture, or because you choose it because it was from a specific place. Feel free to use something else in place of the rock if you have another small item.
- Wear it on a necklace around your neck or wrist, carry it around in your pocket, or keep it in your play area, where you can view it all day.
- Every time you see or touch it, take a moment to express at least one act of gratitude. Just consider one item that

makes you happy or fulfilled, whether it is something tiny like the sun smiling down on you right now or something big like the work that allows you to feed yourself or your family.
- Consider the things you were thankful for throughout the day when you remove the stone from your pockets or off your skin at the end of the day. Repeat this procedure in the morning when you put it on or in your pocket to remind yourself of your gratitude from the previous day.

This will assist you in recalling your blessings and may cause a short period of mindfulness throughout your day. You will be brought into the current moment and out of your thoughts by it, giving you something to concentrate on. Additionally, it might serve as a switch to more optimistic thinking.

2. Jar of Gratitude

Keeping a gratitude jar is a remarkably easy exercise that can greatly impact your happiness and outlook. Only a few ingredients are needed: a jar (a box will also do), ribbon, stamps, sparkle, or whatever else you want to decorate the jar with, paper, a pen or pencil, and appreciation!

Step 1: Look for a box or container.

Step 2: Add any decorations you like to the jar. You can add stickers to the sides, paint the jar, leave it simple, wrap a ribbon around the neck, make it sparkle with transparent glue and glitter, or do anything else to make it attractive.

The ***third*** and most crucial phase will be carried out each day. Throughout the day, consider at least three things for which you are thankful. It might be as simple as a cup of coffee at your favorite spot or as magnificent as the love of a special friend or partner. Do this daily; list your blessings on tiny slips of paper and place them in the jar.

You will eventually discover that you have a jar full of several causes to be grateful for what you have and appreciate the life you are leading. Additionally, it will promote the habit of showing gratitude.

Take a few cards out of the jar if you need a short boost of motivation or are feeling particularly depressed and need a reminder of your blessings.

3. Thankfulness Flower

Start by tracing a circle onto a piece of colored paper.

- Write "Things I'm Thankful for," your name, the name of your family, or even a general thing you're thankful for (such as "my family") on the circle.
- To make flower petals, use a template. You can choose the same hue for a flower that seems more uniformly colored or a variety of colors for one that is colorful and vivid.
- Write your gratitude on the petals of the flower. These can include pleasant weather, having excellent parents, or getting a job.
- To make a flower, adhere or tape these petals to the Centre. This is the bloom of your gratitude!

Mindfulness Activities and Games

(For Teens)

Once you know the most prevalent cognitive distortions, you may begin dedicating a little time each day to finishing the triple column exercise. Even though you can do it in your brain, writing it down will work astonishingly better and help you to silence the critical voice in your head.

How to do it is as follows:

Create three columns on a piece of paper, or launch an Excel or Google Spreadsheet. You can do it whenever you like or when you catch yourself criticizing yourself. Although many individuals I know write theirs before going to bed to unwind, I prefer to write mine in the mornings when I'm most stressed.

Writing down what **Burns,** refers to as your "automatic thought" in the first column. This is your critical inner voice, that nasty, cruel little voice in your head. You are free to be as brief or thorough as you desire.

Read your statement again (reading it aloud always appears a little alarming) and seek for the **cognitive biases** to list in the second column. There can be just one or several. We're using at least four in the scenario: overgeneralization, all-or-nothing thinking, mental filters, and assuming the worst.

Finally, enter your "**logical reaction**" in the third column. You should now rationally consider your feelings and rework your automatic thoughts. You might say, "My presentation could have gone better, but I've had lots of good talks in the past, and I can benefit from this one," using this example. "My supervisor trusted me enough to let me lead the talk, and tomorrow I can discuss how it might have gone more smoothly with her. There is no proof that one bad work day would result in my termination".

You are free to record whatever many or few automatic thoughts you desire. You might not have any after a successful day, and you might need to go through a lot after a significant event or disagreement.

CHAPTER 6
IDENTIFYING THE POSITIVE

(For Teens)

All of your shortcomings and defects are simple to find. If you have poor self-esteem, you store these negative thoughts in your head and eventually find it challenging to see your positive traits.

Every Emotion Is Natural

Imagine that you begin to list every feeling you have ever felt. Try it out right away for fun.

What have you planned?

You have most likely listed emotions like joy, sorrow, excitement, anger, fear, gratitude, pride, confusion, stress, relaxation, and amazement. Then divide your list of feelings into two groups: good emotions and negative emotions.

Being able to experience both pleasant and negative emotions come naturally to us. Even while we may refer to more challenging emotions as "negative," this does not imply that they are undesirable or that we shouldn't feel them. However, the majority of people undoubtedly prefer to experience happy emotions to negative ones. You probably prefer to be joyful than depressed or confident than unsure.

What counts is how well-balanced our emotions are how much of each kind of emotion we feel, whether pleasant or negative. Positive emotions counterbalance negative ones, but they also have other potent advantages. Positive emotions alter our brains in ways that broaden our awareness, attention, and memory instead of narrowing them, as do negative emotions. They enable us to process more information, hold multiple thoughts simultaneously, and comprehend how various ideas are related to one another.

Positive emotions help us see new possibilities, which makes it easier for us to learn new things and advance our talents. As a result, you perform better on assignments and assessments. People who experience good emotions are happier, healthier, more intelligent, and socially adept. So, this chapter aims to help you identifying the positivity in you. Work on the worksheets given in the chapter to discover the **POSITIVE YOU**.

Focus on Solutions, Not on Problems

(For Teens)

When things are difficult, we frequently concentrate on the issues. Problems increase when we concentrate on them; if we do nothing about them, we become sad, impatient, and pessimistic. We will eventually find a solution if we keep an optimistic outlook, have faith that there is a resolution, and keep looking.

Here is a straightforward reality that I discovered many years ago: We amplify what we focus on. This idea has various applications, but in terms of stress, it indicates that if we give our problems too much attention, we will only end up creating additional issues. For instance, I've observed that those always discussing the world's issues seem to draw an unusually high number of personal issues and disappointments into their personal life.

Simply said, negative thinking is the act of directing our attention and mental energy toward problems and things we don't desire. On the other hand, positive thinking is just directing our attention to what is true and what we want. That's all there is to it.

Therefore, acknowledge any issues or problems you're dealing with and recognize that you are dealing with them. The first step in dealing with stressful situations in our lives (after pausing, taking a deep breath, and returning to the present now, of course) is to acknowledge what's happening.

But once you've identified the issue, shift your perspective. Stop saying to yourself, "I don't want this." Alternatively, ask yourself, "This is where I am, but where do I want to be?" Start examining your desires by asking yourself, "What do I want?" "What is the remedy?" What could I do right this second to improve my situation?

Thinking positively does not imply that you will suddenly solve your difficulties. In reality, it's just faith, believing that there are alternatives to our issues and that we are capable of discovering and putting them into action. This is how I think positively, and I find it effective.

Replace Your Negative Thoughts with Positive Thoughts

(For Teens)

Always think optimistic thoughts to counteract any pessimistic ones. Recognize the thoughts running through your head. If they are negative, change your focus to optimistic thoughts. There will probably be internal opposition, and you might even forget to think positive thoughts in their stead. Nevertheless, keep applying this approach until it becomes second nature and effortless.

1. The Two-Column Test

The two-column exercise is a good place to start when you're ready to begin confronting your problematic thoughts. Take a journal, and make two columns in it first. Write down all of your present unfavorable ideas on the left-hand side. Avoid overanalyzing them. Just make as many notes as you can.

Write one to three counterarguments in the right-hand column. This can assist you in separating yourself from the aspect of your mind, or inner critic, that generates the automatic ideas while "You" are noticing them and doing the therapeutic job. Put your negative thoughts within quote marks. This might encourage you to start thinking of them as ideas rather than unquestionable truths, like the thousands of other ideas that cross your head daily.

2. Find Fresh Proof

In our minds, we have amassed evidence contributing to our unhelpful thoughts. Our past experiences teach us valuable lessons about the world around us as well as ourselves. However, if you find yourself starting to think those negative things are true, it's time to look for some new proof. On your phone, set a timer for the same time each day. When it sounds, list five qualities about yourself or your work that you admire in your head, out loud, or on paper.

3. Reduce The Impact

When you see yourself having a negative thought, pause and ask yourself:

Would I utter this to another person aloud?

What would I say to a young child?

Would I allow my child to be addressed in that manner?

Sometimes, all it takes to change anything is to picture what someone else would think if they knew what you were thinking. This might encourage you to use language that is more loving. Speaking up for yourself may be empowering. You can tell your brain, "Hey, I don't like how you talk to me. I've heard enough from you. I'm through.

4. Practice Accepting Yourself

In addition to having unfavorable ideas, you could also feel guilty for thinking such things in the first place. Creating resistance to your current reality can exacerbate your internal anguish. Simply take note of any negative thoughts that come to mind. Wait a moment. Do your best to resist pushing it away. Do you have the ability to let it exist here?

Repeat Affirmations

(For Teens)

When faced with challenging or unpleasant circumstances, repeat a positive affirmation. Positive remarks called affirmations can uplift and inspire you and alter your mood. Repeating positive affirmations to oneself regularly might help your brain accept them as true. Your behaviors frequently follow when you genuinely believe you can accomplish a goal.

Affirmations can help you feel more at ease before the interview, and being confident in your readiness can also help you avoid self-defeating ideas or actions that could hinder your success. Keep in mind that taking action is essential.

You still need to take action on your own, but repeating an affirmation might help you feel more motivated and confident. Consider affirmations as the first step toward change rather than the change itself. Think about the friend who always wants to know about your private life. You don't want to say anything that would upset them, but you also don't want to engage in a conversation with them.

When you begin to feel your blood boil, an affirmation like "I can stay cool even when I feel annoyed" could help you develop the habit of breathing exercises or grounding exercises. You can use these strategies, together with your affirmations, to help you get through the difficult situation until you can gracefully leave.

Do Not Take Anything Too Personally

(For Teens)

Try not to take personally what other people say or think about you. There is no justification in the world for letting their opinions damage you. It is you who permits their ideas and statements to have an impact on your emotions. People frequently do not even realize they have harmed you.

Do not consider what was stated or the reasons behind it. You may have misconstrued what they meant or meant something else. They might be joking, or their remarks may not have been about you.

Learn to let go of your anger, resentment, and injured sentiments. This is made possible with just a slight amount of emotional detachment, another word for letting go.

Keep it Positive

(For Teens)

Read the situations and answer accordingly.

Keep it Positive

Situation: All the kids in your class want to sit next to Jeannie
Negative Thought: No one ever wants to sit next to me because I don't have clothes like Jeannie.

Positive Thought: _____
_____

Situation: My family and I are driving to the amusement park
Negative Thought: We are probably going to get there late because I'm sure there will be traffic.

Positive Thought: _____
_____

Situation: Your teacher compliments your 100% on your spelling test.
Negative Thought: Anyone could get a 100. They give us the words beforehand.

Positive Thought: _____
_____

Positively Wonderful

(For Teens)

Can you tell some positive things about you?

Positively Wonderful

I am good at .....

- _____
- _____
- _____

Positive thoughts I had this week

- _____
- _____
- _____

I am proud that I .....

- _____
- _____
- _____

My teacher thinks I am .....

- _____

Positive Thinking Please

(For Teens)

Positive Thinking Please

Complete the sentences with a "positive" ending in the example.

1. The test will be hard but_____

_____

_____

1. I'll succeed it_____

_____

_____

1. No matter what happens, I'll_____

_____

_____

1. I may not be perfect but_____

_____

_____

1. Sometimes I have days like theirs but_____

_____

_____

1. Even though I'm disappointed, I'll_____

_____

_____

Optimism

(For Teens)

Optimism

Describe what optimistic behavior looks like?

_____
_____
_____
_____

What is meant by positive self talk?

_____
_____
_____
_____
_____

In What ways are you optimistic?

_____
_____
_____
_____

Optimism Sheet 2

(For Teens)

Optimism

1. Provide a time where you made the best out of a difficult or trying situation.
2. How is optimism similar to having a positive attitude?
3. Why is it important to be optimistic?
4. Optimism is a choice, explain this.
5. Why should you think positive thoughts about yourself and others?
6. How do you feel when you are around people who are negative?

Positive Affirmation

(For Teens)

I have already discussed the importance of affirmations. Now create your own.

Positive Affirmations

A positive affirmation is something spoken aloud that you want to believe or want it to be true. Repeating positive affirmations daily can help shift your internal dialogue from negative to positive. Create your own affirmations!

1. *I trust myself to make the best decision for me.*
2. *I matter and what I have to offer this world matters.*
3. _____
4. _____
5. _____
6. _____
7. _____
8. _____
9. _____
10. _____
11. _____
12. _____
13. _____
14. _____
15. _____
16. _____
17. _____

My Daily Affirmations

(For Teens)

Complete the sentences.

 **My Daily Affirmations**
Reflect, Release, Declare, & Conquer

I am ....

_____
_____
_____

I am worthy of ....

_____
_____
_____

I will ....

_____
_____
_____

I let go of ....

_____
_____
_____

I appreciate ....

_____
_____
_____

Today I will ....

_____
_____
_____

10 Minutes to Recognize Good Stuff

(For Teens)

10 MINUTES TO RECOGNIZE THE GOOD STUFF

Things, people, and places you adore.

One thing you have worked hard to achieve:
_____

One things that's going well right now:

[ ]

Two subjects or pursuits you're passionate about:
_____   _____

Two people you can count on for warm hugs and kinds words:
_____   _____

Three things to look forward for

Mindfulness Activities and Games

(For Teens)

You can do these five quick and simple workouts every day to feel positively. Parents and Teachers can also use this exercise.

1. Take Five Minutes to Observe a Leaf

All you need for this practice is a leaf and your focus. Take a leaf in your hand, pick it up, and focus solely on it for five minutes. Take note of the patterns, hues, shapes, textures, and colors. Doing so will make you aware of the moment and connect your thoughts with what is happening right now.

2. Four Minutes of Mindful Dining

This practice requires conscious eating. Be mindful of what you are holding and how it feels in your hands. Bring your attention to the fragrance once you have taken note of the texture, weight, color, etc. Finally, start eating, but take your time and pay close attention. Take note of the flavor and how it feels on your tongue. This practice could encourage you to try unfamiliar cuisines.

3. Pay Attention to your Ideas for 15 Minutes

This mindfulness practice, which is a mainstay, aims to improve the attention of your ideas. To start, find a comfortable posture to sit or lie down in and try to allow any tension to leave your body. Prioritize your breathing, shift your attention to how your body feels, and turn to your thoughts. Recognize the thoughts that cross your mind, but repress the temptation to categorize or condemn them. Imagine them as a vanishing cloud in your mental sky. When an idea causes your mind to stray, notice what has caught your attention and gently nudge it back into your thoughts.

4. Five-Minute Mindfulness Bell Exercise

To begin this practice, close your eyes and wait for the cue while listening. Your goal is to concentrate on the sound as soon as you hear it and keep doing so until it stops entirely. You can do this practice to help you stay rooted in the present.

5. Focus On the Center

Concentrating your attention on the center of the changing color pattern is a straightforward objective. You can allow your mind to wander freely while being in the present and observing any thoughts that arise. This practice can help you focus and think deeply, but be careful not to become lost in your ideas. Instead, try to stay in the present and let your thoughts drift.

CHAPTER 7
IMPROVING PHYSICAL HEALTH

(For Teens)

There is much more to a person's total health than just the lack of illness, the state of being physically, mentally, and socially healthy. Ultimately, it's the secret to leading a fruitful and fulfilling life.

Ways to get Better Health

The idea of health can be divided into several areas. These could encompass behavioral, emotional, mental, and physical wellness. Any person can take action to maintain their health in these areas. There are some things you should pay extra attention to as a teenager.

Physical Condition: Maintaining Your Body

Regular exercise: Teenagers should engage in physical activity for at least 60 minutes daily.

Adopt a balanced diet. Eating well is crucial to your development and growth. Eat a range of protein-rich foods, whole grains, fruits, vegetables, and low-fat dairy products. Even as a teen, avoid junk food like soda, fast food, and chips. You will benefit from this as you age.

Keep a healthy weight. Obesity in adults is more likely to occur in children and teenagers. They are also more vulnerable to bullying, despair, and other chronic ailments.

Get adequate rest. Teenagers typically require between 9 and 9 ½ hours of sleep every night. Many people only work an average of seven hours. Your capacity for concentration and academic performance are both significantly impacted by sleep.

Children with additional requirements should engage in physical activity regularly, despite their inherent limitations. Numerous organized activities have been changed or encouraged so these kids can participate. Additionally, certain playgrounds have been created with unique equipment and sensory activities. This promotes play among kids of different skill levels.

To meet your child's needs, your family might also try scheduling time for physical activity. To maintain a healthy body, you should also refrain from mental conditions that create issues. This chapter will be focusing on maintaining a healthy body by having a healthy schedule during a day.

Set A Goal

(For Parents/Teachers)

Get your child's opinion on a target they'd like to achieve while discussing physical activity's advantages. A child might be inspired to move and develop lifelong healthy habits by achieving small milestones.

Goals can include going for a daily stroll, improving the quantity of leaping jacks or squats they can perform, extending the time they can maintain a plank. Online, you may find a variety of fitness challenges for people of various ages and levels of fitness. Think about hanging a chart in your home to mark off daily accomplishments and track progress.

Get Creative

(For Parents/Teachers)

Variety is essential for keeping exercise enjoyable for kids. To ensure that your child enjoys physical activity, find out the things they prefer to do. Change it daily, whether walking, biking, dancing, interval running, yoga, outdoor play, bodyweight workouts, or something else. Write various exercises on paper, fold and draw them out of a basket as a lucky draw and decide who in the family picks one activity for the day.

As adolescence approaches, kids frequently experience self-consciousness and become cautious about moving outside of their comfort zone. It's never too late to re-inspire them, so all is not lost!

1. Set a Good Example

Leading by example is the best approach to support your teen's creativity. Maybe you previously had a love for writing or enjoyed dabbling in painting, but regrettably, it was buried behind the responsibilities of family life. Or perhaps you attend your pottery class without failing every week. Whether you love to bake, decorate your home, or have a passion for arithmetic (yes, that counts, too), do it with vigor and show your teen.

2. It Goes Beyond Arts & Crafts

Writing and art aren't the only forms of creativity. It also has to do with having creative ideas and the capacity to employ imagination in everyday situations. For instance, if your adolescent is having trouble with a certain portion of their schoolwork, utilize different techniques to spark their imagination, such as creativity, to come up with answers to their difficulties and encourage them to think creatively. Use team-building activities as a family, or inspire your teenagers to work with friends and peers on a project. Productively exchanging views and ideas on a subject helps foster creativity.

3. Encourage Inquiry

Encourage your teenagers to ask questions about anything they are unsure of and hunt up the answers to foster creativity. Let them explore their thoughts and opinions to learn that not everyone feels the same way they do and that's okay. Show them that because they hold a different opinion than others, that doesn't make it bad, while at the same time, teach your teen that there are polite and respectful ways to voice their opinions.

4. Avoid Stifling Their Imagination

Encourage your teenagers to try something new, possibly a hobby they haven't thought about before, like picking up a musical instrument. Allow them to select their dinner menu, and encourage them to select a dish they have never tried. Avoid imposing your personal opinions too blatantly; even the most well-intentioned parent can unintentionally kill their teen's originality by being excessively controlling. Back off if you find yourself becoming sarcastic or dismissive of your teen's most absurd ideas or proposals or if you are more concerned with the mess they are creating. It's hard to be creative when your parent is a neurotic, hovering nag.

5. Show Them That Taking Risks is Acceptable.

As children grow into teenagers, the propensity to take chances frequently becomes stunted. It can be frightening for them to consider trying something new or engaging in an activity outside their comfort zone because they are much more intensely aware of the harsh environment around them. It's crucial to promote the idea that failing at the first attempt is OK; failure can result from inventiveness, but that's fine. You can't succeed if you don't attempt.

6. Understand Life

Nature is the best source of inspiration. Take your teenagers to the beach or on a stroll in the woods. Encourage your children to pay attention to their surroundings by stopping to appreciate a beautiful flower or the complex artwork created by nature on an old tree trunk. Take a deep breath and simply enjoy the beauty around you.

Visit museums and galleries to fully immerse them in history, culture, and the arts. Take them to a ballet performance, a musical performance, or a fine-dining restaurant for dinner. A culturally conscious youngster exposed to variety is much more receptive to being creatively inspired. There is a huge universe waiting to be discovered.

Make Exercise a Family Priority

(For Parents/Teachers)

It is better to lead by example if you want to motivate your youngster to exercise genuinely. What their family is doing is the main thing that can affect if kids are going to thrive and be active. Instead of expecting your children to exercise independently, choose to be active with them as much as feasible.

Go for a family stroll or bike ride, play some soccer outside, or accompany your kid to a yoga or workout. When your youngster sets a goal, make a goal of your own to set an example of good behavior. Exercise improves your family's health and provides priceless bonding time.

Jumping Jacks Game

(For Parents/Teachers)

How to Play

- Put your feet together and your arms by your sides with your elbows straight.
- Step apart and jump while raising your arms above your head.
- Over your head, clap your hands collectively.
- Jump your feet and bring your arms back to your sides.
- Do not stop breathing.

Exercises like jumping jacks are effective. Performing these activities promotes:

- Cardiopulmonary conditioning
- Physical exercise
- Cooperation
- Timing
- Motor skills
- Strength training
- Rhythmic vestibular input

Physical Activity through Games

(For Parents/Teachers)

What are some exercises that can assist your youngster in honing this ability? To name a few:

Toe taps: Have your youngster touch their toe on an area you've placed in front of them. Turn it into a game by calling numbers and seeing how many they can complete. Alternately, use both the left and right feet. You can perform this on the ground or higher height for a more difficult variation. The target can also be moved from directly in front to diagonally to the side.

Grab a ball and have your youngster try to **balance** while keeping one foot on top of it while holding the ball. If you want to see who can endure the longest, time them or have two individuals try it simultaneously. Make sure you alternate your feet. Larger, stiffer balls are more difficult to balance than soft, squishy ones.

Popping bubbles: Which child doesn't enjoy popping bubbles? This activity is enjoyable. Have them attempt to stomp on bubbles to make them pop by blowing bubbles!

Stepping over barriers: Have your youngster attempt to cross a space while stepping over barriers that stand in their way. You can use anything you can think of, such as puzzle books, wooden paddles, toys, and food. Taller and wider are harder than shorter and narrower. Additionally, ensure that the obstacle is solid and not a sphere that will roll away from someone who runs into it. Additionally, you might use painter's tape to create obstructions in your hallway that require people to step over the tape of different heights.

One of yoga poses is the **tree posture**. Kids enjoy copying it, and if the knee part seems too difficult, they can "cheat" by placing their foot close to the other foot.

Fill Up a Balloon and Don't Let It Touch the Ground Game

(For Parents/Teachers)

1. Protect your Balloon

Excellent for bigger gatherings of five or more people. Give each youngster a balloon and a string that measures about a meter in length. Their balloon should be inflated before being tied to a string and wrapped around their ankle. Supervision is necessary.

2. Balloon Race

It is a two- or more-player outdoor activity. Place a balloon below their legs, have them begin at the start position, and race to the end zone without losing or exploding the balloon. The races can be completed in relays if you have a big number and a small area.

3. The Balloon Game

Organize your children into even groupings and have them sit in parallel lines, each child about half a meter apart, if you have at least 10. Give the recipient a blown-up balloon. After you give the signal to begin, the teams must pass the balloon under the next person's knees and over their heads until it reaches the person at the front of the line. The winning team is the first to hold its balloon up at the front of the line.

Developing Core Stability Games

(For Parents/Teachers)

The growth of the hip/pelvic and trunk muscles, which stabilize, align, and move the body's trunk and establish a solid foundation before we move, is known as core stability. Your child should work on developing core stability since it creates a solid basis for many other functional skills, including balance, and gross and fine motor skills, among many others.

Animal Walks: A quick and simple exercise that combines gross motor abilities like agility, balance, core strength, and crossing the midline.

With your stomach on the ground, perform a commando crawl, using your arms and legs to propel your body forward. Try going under a chair or through a tunnel of couch cushions, etc., or over mounds of pillows.

Crawling: Get practice on soft surfaces such as mounds of cushions. Practice walking on your knees while moving forward, backward, or sideways. The muscles that surround the hips and pelvis, which are necessary for proper balance, are strengthened by this exercise.

Hold your child at the knees or legs as they walk while using a wheelbarrow. Watch for core muscle fatigue, such as a drooping back or excessive hip bending. You can start holding the legs at the shins, then move on to the ankles if your youngster performs well and doesn't exhibit these indicators of exhaustion.

Healthy Habits

(For Teens)

Match sentences with correct pictures. Indicate whether the activity is healthy or not.

Healthy Habits

Healthy Habits Game

(For Teens)

Physical Activity

(For Teens)

Physical Activity

1. Tick the children who are doing physical activity.

2. This boy is **playing basketball,** so his **heartbeat** ☐

and his **breathing** ☐

3. This girl was running but now she is **resting.**

so her **heartbeat** ☐

and his **breathing** ☐

Staying Healthy

(For Teens)

Can you fill in the blanks?

Staying healthy

Use your creativity to fill in the blanks

_____ or _____ can't help you to stay fit.

_____ will make you fit. You can _____ or _____ or _____ if you don't like team sports.

Regular exercise gives you more_____

_____ and _____ contain too much sugar, fat or salt

_____ and _____ help you to stay healthy and grow strong.

_____ drinks contain a lot of sugar.

One_____ of _____ contains 9 teaspoons of sugar.

Your body needs calcium to make healthy_____

READ.

I don't like vegetables, I like having pizza, crisps and hot dogs for lunch. I don't eat fish at all. Sometimes Mum makes me drink some milk. I don't drink fizzy drinks. Every day I walk to school. I go swimming every week. I also ride my bike in the park at weekends.	I eat lots of fruits and vegetables to stay healthy. I usually have chicken with rice and salad for lunch. I also drink lots of milk because it keeps my bones and teeth strong. I don't like water very much so I often drink fizzy drinks. I can't ride a bike so my Mum drives me to school every day.

Health and Wellness Check

(For Teens)

Write your healthy routine below.

Health & Wellness Check

Monday

Exercise:

Healthy Foods:

Mindfulness:

Social Connections:

Tuesday

Exercise:

Healthy Foods:

Mindfulness:

Social Connections:

Self-Care Activity

(For Teens)

Select what you feel and what should you do.

Today's Self-Care

I Feel	I Should
Stressed	Try to Relax
Sad	Ask for Help
Angry	Think before I act
Upset	Talk to someone
Anxious	Write down my worries
Lonely	Do something creative
Hopeless	Help someone in need
Overwhelmed	Pray or meditate

My Wellness Plan

My Wellness Plan

Warning Signs: The things you might notice when you start feeling overwhelmed or trustrated	**Places I Can Go; Things I Can Do:** Think about the places you can go or things you can do where you feel most comfortable and list these here
Family and Friends I Can Talk To: Write down the names of family members and friends who can support you, include how they can help	**Community Resources I Can Access:** This can include community services agencies, a counsellor you feel comfortable with, doctor, recreation activities and more
Online Support I Can Apps: This can include online support groups, opps, etc	**Emergency Phone Number:** Write down who you can call in an emergency, Include your local crisis line, as well as any crisis program for children and youth that may be in your community

You can do ANYTHING, but not EVERTHING

CHAPTER 8

BECOMING MORE ASSERTIVE

(For Teens)

Being assertive is a good method of communication. It is the capacity to stand up for ourselves honestly and respectfully. Being aggressive can be helpful in various daily circumstances, such as asking someone out on a date, addressing a teacher with a query, or performing well.

Not everyone has a natural tendency toward assertiveness. Some people use an overly passive style of communication. Some people's styles are overly combative. The ideal stance between these two is assertive. We can accomplish our goals with the support of an assertive communication approach. But assertiveness goes further than that; it demonstrates our respect for both ourselves and other people.

Speaking firmly conveys that the person believes in oneself. They understand the value of their thoughts and feelings.

How can you determine your assertiveness level?

Here are a few instances:

Paola has a passive fashion sense. Paola is most likely to respond, "I don't know – what do you want to see?" if you ask her what movie she wants to see. Normally, she defers others' judgment but regrets not expressing her preferences. She finds it annoying that her buddies chat so much. Paola tries to join the conversation but talks so gently that people accidentally talk over her.

Jaini has a too assertive manner. Speaking her mind is no problem for Jaini. However, she comes out as brash and opinionated when she does. Jaini controls the conversation, speaks out frequently, and pays little attention. She will let you know if she disagrees with you, usually with sarcasm or a putdown. She is known for being insensitive and pushy.

Benni has a commanding demeanor. Benni is honest when he responds to your request for his opinion. He will express his disagreement with you, if necessary, but he will do it without demeaning you or making you feel guilty. Benni is also curious about other's viewpoint. He pays attention to what you say. Benni seems to accept your point of view even when he disagrees with you.

Thus, balancing assertiveness is an important life skill. This chapter will help you to be assertive and polite in your conversation.

Building A Healthy Self-Perception

(For Teens)

Self-image is the subjective perception or mental image we have of ourselves. Self-image is an "internal dictionary" that lists traits about the self, including intelligence, ability, beauty, and traits like selfishness and kindness. These traits serve as a collective depiction of our strengths and limitations, as seen by us. You can develop a healthy self-perception by;

- Doing a self-image assessment.
- Making a list of all your good traits.
- Getting your loved ones to list your good characteristics.
- Setting attainable, quantifiable goals and objectives for yourself.
- Confronting your biases in thinking.
- Recognizing and investigating the effects of labels from childhood.
- Avoiding comparing yourself to other people.
- Cultivating your strengths.
- Mastering the art of self-love.
- Making good affirmations.
- Keeping in mind that you are special.
- Keeping in mind your progress.

Self-Talk for Assertiveness

(For Teens)

Self-talk is important for defining identity. Self-talk is having constant thoughts to ourselves. When you feel down, what do you tell yourself?

- Make an error? (I cannot do this, or, I'm stupid.)
- Succeed at a challenging task? (I'm fairly smart, or wow, I was lucky.)
- Obtain admiration? ("Thanks, I love it too," or "It's simply an old shirt I bought from the shop.")
- Fail? ('I'll never be able to achieve this,' or 'Alright, that method didn't work; what other options are there?)

People who send themselves affirming messages on their accomplishments (such as "Yahoo - I did it! It demonstrates that I am capable") blame failure on external factors. ("It's nothing personal, just a terrible hair day for him.") By utilizing self-talk that validates our identity, we either positively or negatively support our self-esteem.

Your beliefs about yourself will change if you actively control your self-talk. Additionally, you will see that your behavior has changed because beliefs influence actions. You'll gain

Planning What You Are Talking About

(For Teens)

Your confidence will increase, and you'll seem more assertive if you are knowledgeable about the issue and clear about what you desire to say. Every effective communication begins with having "something valuable to say, and your goal is to re-create your fundamental concept within your audience's heads.

This requires that you:

- Concentrate on a single important concept.
- Determine what will make people care.
- Build the notion around ideas that the audience already knows.

After all, effective communication requires that you have something to say.

Self-Evaluation for Assertiveness

(For Teens)

Communication is influenced by how you see yourself. Based on how you interact and speak with others, the self-evaluation questions below help you determine if you have issues with assertiveness. You just need to answer with Yes or No.

Statements	Yes	No
Do you have confidence? Or do your phrases contain too many pauses, ums, and errs?		
How do you interact with others, whether standing or sitting?		
Do you stand straight, or stare down?		
Do you give people your full attention when you speak to them?		
Can you ask questions you have, or do you avoid doing so?		
When speaking, do you project your voice? Are you audible and speaking clearly?		
Do you feel at ease among other people?		
Do you feel confident declining requests?		
Can you disagree with what is being said even if you hold a different viewpoint or beliefs?		
If applicable, can you demonstrate your annoyance?		
Can you defend yourself when accused of doing something you didn't do?		

2 or 3 "no" responses indicate that you are probably confident and do not have any trouble expressing your requirements and wants.

You probably have a bad opinion of yourself if you answer "no" four to six times. It's harder for you to express what you need and want.

If you answer "no" seven times or more, you probably have trouble being forceful, believe you don't deserve respect and are prone to giving in.

Assertive Talk

(For Teens)

Always take into account what other people are hearing when speaking assertively. Speaking slurred or unclearly will make you sound unconfident and unpassionate. Playing back prior communications might help determine how they might have been enhanced if these communication strategies had been used more frequently.

Worksheet

Seek out opportunities to put the four strategies into practice, then refine them in light of your learnings. Examine the following techniques to comprehend how the way you use language affects your ability to seem assertive:

1. Use simple, straightforward statements to make your needs and wants to be known.

Example: You get a call when you are departing your home in the evening to meet friends. I'm glad to hear from you, but I must go now. Do you mind if I call you tomorrow?

2. Demonstrate empathy while defending your rights by demonstrating that you are mindful of the other person's predicament.

Example: Although I know your hectic schedule, we must meet tomorrow to discuss the project's problems.

(When a conversation contains conflict, or you are uncomfortable expressing a question, showing empathy can be a helpful way to interact with someone.)

3. Escalation: It is an essential ability for increasingly difficult and combative interactions.

There are instances when it may be important to become more assertive while maintaining composure and control. For instance, when the other person disregards your demands or your rights.

4. "I" or "Me": Once you've made it obvious what the other person did, express your displeasure.

<u>Example</u>: I disagree with the new timetables because they disregard X.

Instead of beginning with a more accusatory "You" remark, describe how this has made you feel or affected you. It sounds less combative or contentious and is harder to dispute.

5 Exercises for Assertiveness

(For Teens)

You may need to develop new habits to be more forceful. While implementing numerous changes at once can be difficult, doing so gradually may be more comfortable.

Think about the following:

- Be specific about your goals.

What do you hope to achieve? Make an extended vision.

- Set objectives.

Set SMART (Specified, Measured, Achievable, Related, and Time limited) objectives for the near term that will assist you in achieving your long-term objectives.

- Engage in some imagination and optimistic thinking.

Think about your ideal selves and your preferred communication style. You can increase your self-confidence and respect for yourself by redefining your self-perception.

- Put yourself to the test.

One can develop growth and confidence by addressing and overcoming difficulties and hurdles.

- Think about your advantages.

Utilize your strengths by being aware of them.

Passive, Aggressive, and Assertive Communication

(For Teens)

Passive:

- "I wish I could play with them."
- "Nobody likes me."
- "They should invite me to play."
- "She's so mean."
- "She doesn't think about me."

Assertive:

- "Can I play with you?"
- "May I play with you?"
- "What are you playing?"
- "Would you like to play _____?"
- "What would you like to do?"

Aggressive:

- Using a very loud voice
- "That is so sick."
- "You're so mean." You're horrible."
- "You're disgusting."
- "That's is stupid game any way. Who cares to play?"
- "You're so dumb."
- "Oh be quiet, You are talking too much."
- "On you're totally wrong. That's not how it goes"

Passive, Aggressive, and Assertive

(For Teens)

I have already given some examples of passive, aggressive and assertive communication. Here are some scenarios. Write statements accordingly.

Passive, Aggressive, and Assertive Communication

Scenario	Your boss asks you to stay late, while everyone else leaves. You're always the one who stays late, and tonight you have plans
Passive	
Aggressive	
Assertive	

Scenario	Your partner left a mess in the kitchen, and you're too busy to clean.
Passive	
Aggressive	
Assertive	

Scenario	You're at a restaurant, and the server brought you the wrong dish.
Passive	
Aggressive	
Assertive	

Scenario	A friend showed up at your house uninvited, Usually you would be happy to let them in, but this time you're busy.
Passive	
Aggressive	
Assertive	

Asking Help

(For Teens)

In assertive communication, asking for help in polite and understandable sentences is important. Here is another exercise for you. Look at the scenario and choose what you should do. Think of a problem and give your answer.

Practice Asking for Help

Scenario
You're not Finished copying down the notes and you need more time to finish

Gaining Attetion
☐ Say the person's name
☐ Raise your hand
☐ _____

State the Problem
The problem is_____
_____

☐ I struggle.   ☐ I don't know.
☐ It is difficult for me.   ☐ It is hard for me.

How you Tried to Solve the Problem
I have_____
_____

☐ tried   ☐ asked
☐ used   ☐ read

What you need the person to do
Can_____
_____

☐ I please   ☐ you please
☐ I have   ☐ I lock

(All the exercises and activities below are for Teachers/Parents)

Standing Up for Yourself

Play out a scenario when one youngster tries to steal something from another forcefully. Explain to the child that playing with something doesn't have to be immediately start sharing. Together, come up with a list of polite, forceful methods for them to stand up for themselves.

Meeting New People

Teach your kid how to meet new people. Ask if they have played in the past with others whom they met the first time. Practice being a new kid in a group of friends.

Making Mistakes

Children should learn how to manage the issue when they make mistakes. Such issues not only cause stress but can also undermine a person's confidence. Play out and address problematic scenarios. Talk about how to be truthful about what occurred (a broken vase or being unable to complete a task), and if necessary, apologize or put a stop to it from happening again.

PART-III

EMOTIONS REGULATION SKILLS

(For Teachers/Parents)

Self-regulation is now considered to play a crucial role in fostering well-being throughout life, including physical, emotional, social, and economic health and academic success. Self-regulation controls one's thoughts and feelings to do goal-directed behaviors, such as the several steps required for success in the classroom, interpersonal interactions, and future opportunities. Better self-regulation implies higher success rate, greater financial planning, less risky behaviors like substance use and aggression, and lower health expenditures. Supporting the development of self-regulation in teens is an investment in society.

Although many self-regulation-related programs for older teenagers and young adults focus on "soft skills," "life skills," and resilience-building, using a particular self-regulation framework may be advantageous for 14 to 18-year-olds. Exercises, worksheets and activities can assist self-regulation with the promising practices and theoretical ideas offered in this part.

From infancy through early adulthood, self-regulation is developed and learned through interactions with caregivers and the surrounding environment (and beyond). Like teaching literacy, cognitive, emotional, and behavioral self-regulation abilities can be taught over time. Effective interventions can reinforce and improve abilities even for young people; there are continual possibilities for intervention throughout development. To help your kid to develop emotions regulation skill, the third part of this book will provide you guidance and some simple strategies. Have a look at these.

CHAPTER 9
STRESS MANAGEMENT SKILLS

(For Teens)

If you experience significant stress on a daily basis, your general health is in danger. Stress has a detrimental effect on your physical and emotional health. Your ability to think clearly, perform successfully, and enjoying yourself is compromised. It could seem as though there is nothing you can do to relax. The bills won't stop coming in, the hours in the day won't increase, and your duties to your family and job will always be demanding. You actually have a lot more control than you would think.

Effective emotion regulation enables you to loosen the hold stress has on your life, enabling you to be happier, better, and more productive. The ultimate goal is to have a balanced life with enough time for work, relationships, leisure, and pleasure as well as the resilience to handle stress and confront challenges head-on. However, there is no one approach to managing stress or learning regulatory abilities. This chapter is an experiment to find the solution that best suits your needs. Work on the exercises for controlling your emotions listed below to get there.

Talk About Your Problems

(For Teens)

Numerous life situations can occasionally leave us feeling too emotional. We move around feeling tense and emotionally heated during these moments. Often, we cannot undo what has happened to us, such as when a loved one passes away, a horrible accident occurs, or we discover suffering from a severe illness. We feel emotionally paralyzed when these sensations hit us. We discover ourselves imprisoned in a state of anguish and despair. Talking about your problems with a loved one can be helpful at these moments.

The phrase catharsis best describes the benefit of conversing. Speaking causes a catharsis or a sense of relief. Our internally-charged feelings start to de-charge. Nothing in our lives could change our pain into happiness, but discussing can help to lessen some of the suffering, which makes us comfortable.

Go Easy on Yourself

(For Teens)

Here are some suggestions to help you take it easy on yourself during these challenging times if you feel worn out and foggy-headed.

⁂ Observe the Effect

How is the present circumstance affecting you? How does it manifest for you if you're having trouble?

Maybe it's a lack of vigor, sensitivity to emotions, excessive anxiety, impatience, a sense of being on edge, or a desire to withdraw and seal off. What mood are you in? How does it feel inside of you?

Feelings include heaviness, dizziness, jitters, headaches, bodily aches, restlessness, or other unpleasant feelings.

⁂ Laugh

Our sense of humor departs when we are on edge due to stress and uncertainty. A good laugh helps ease the tension. Watch humorous animal videos, put on your favorite comedy, or make a phone call. And check if you can decide to be happier rather than disappointed or irritated (with yourself or others) when anything goes wrong.

⁂ Connect

Maybe you've been holding virtual gatherings with your loved ones every day of the week, or maybe you've withdrawn into yourself. In either case, keeping in touch and interacting with the people we care about is essential.

Eliminate Your Triggers

(For Teens)

It can be difficult to manage if you don't know what's generating your stress. Finding the source of your stress is the first step in managing it for this reason. Once you know your triggers, you can take precautions to avoid them or develop a coping mechanism for when stress overwhelms you.

Try journaling for a week if you're unsure what stresses you out. You can determine when you were most stressed out and the events surrounding it by looking back on the entire week. Your interests are good indication of how you should manage stress. Those pastimes are the ones that naturally make you happy, free from social obligations or the demands of your never-ending to-do list.

Exercise. Moving your body greatly impacts your stress levels, whether you walk, jog, swim, perform, cycle, or perform yoga. Exercise lowers levels of the stress response (such as cortisol and adrenaline) and releases potent endorphins into the brain, which improve mood, promote relaxation, and serve as natural painkillers.

Meditate. Stress can be successfully treated with meditation. It assists in ridding your mind of stressful ideas and fostering a tranquil state of mind that persists long after a meditation session. It can also be done anywhere, anytime. It only requires five minutes.

Be imaginative. A great way to decompress is through the arts. Any form of creative expression, including painting, knitting, carpentry, coloring, sculpture, and photography, can lower stress. Research has shown that after 45 minutes of creative engagement, people's cortisol (the stress hormone) levels are significantly lower.

Take a book or music class. You can get away from your troubles and daily anxieties by losing yourself in a wonderful novel or a favorite album. Escapism, in this way, diverts the intellect and activates the imagination.

Spend some time outside. Immersing yourself in nature has been demonstrated to provide a variety of health advantages, including lower blood pressure, reduced stress, and elevated mood. Not a fan of nature? To improve your mental health, spend just two hours outdoors each week.

Causes of Stress

What causes stress? While there are many answers. Most stressors are related to one (or more) of these four categories.

T — THREAT to SELF-ESTEEM/EGO
Something that may be damaging to how you see yourself or how others see you

O — OUT of NOWHERE
Something you had no way of knowing would happen

N — NEW or DIFFERENT
Something you have not experienced before

S — SENSE of CONTROL
Something you have little or no control over

what is causing your stress, you can figure out strategies to manage it effectively.

Stress and My Body

(For Teens)

Color in the reactions that happen to your body when you are feeling sad or depressed.

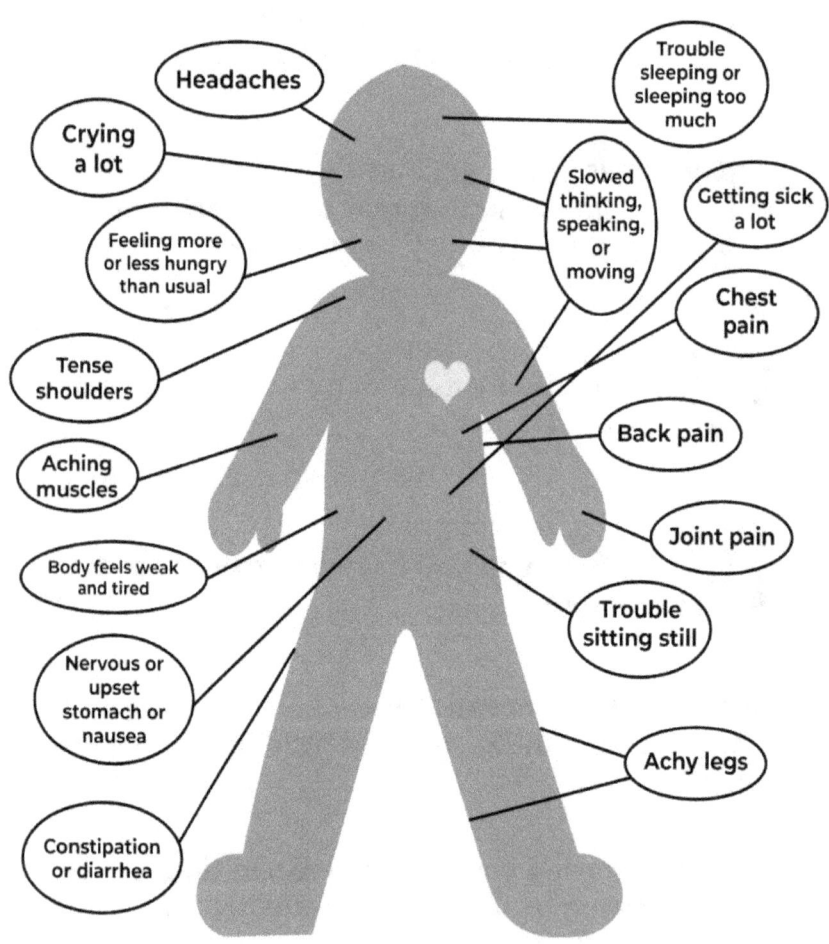

That Stressed Me Out

(For Teens)

That Really Stressed Me Out

Read through the situations below and ✓ each one that you experienced within the last year. Mark whether the situation led to good stress or bad stress.

Situation	I experienced this within the last year	Good Stress (situation motivated you to prepare and do your best)	Bad Stress (situation made you feel overwhelmed and worried most of the time).
1. Meeting new people			
2. Being peer pressured			
3. Fighting with friends or siblings			
4. Failing a test			
5. Giving a presentation			
6. Engaged in several activities			
7. Parents arguing			
8. Feeling left out			
9. Moving			
10. Being teased			

If you have checked the 'bad stress' box more than three times, you might be experiencing stress overload. Talk to a trusted adult.

My Stress Triggers

(For Teens)

Write down in circles what causes you stress. Color the most commonly occurred triggers "Red".

My Stress Triggers

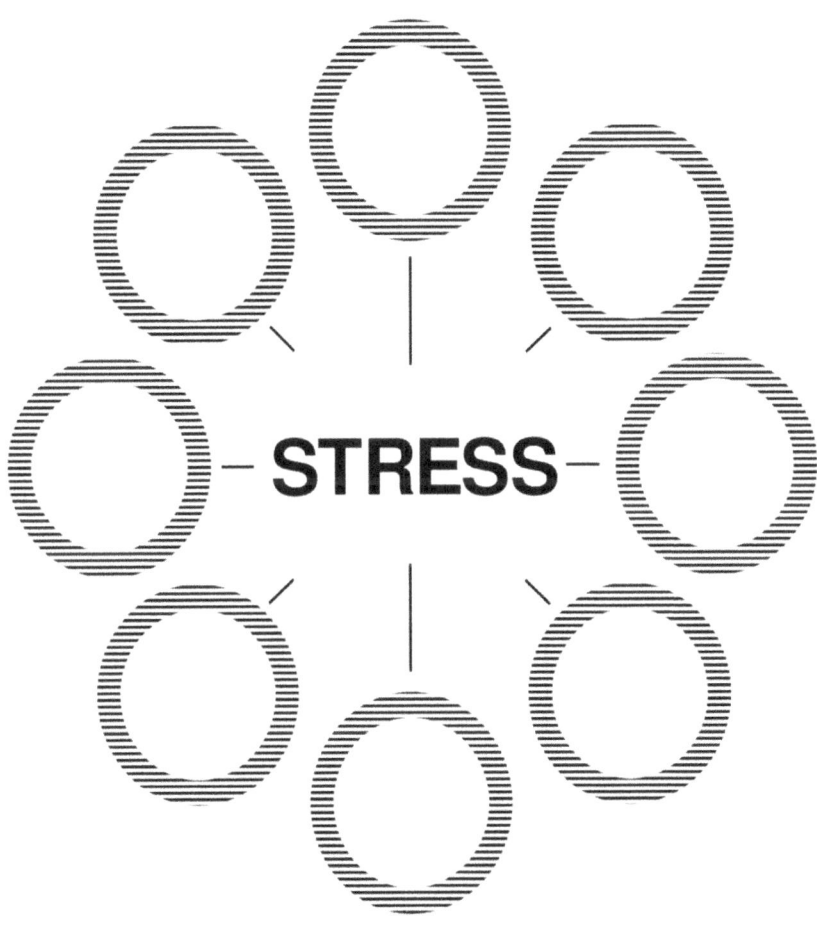

Recognizing Stress

(For Teens)

Recognizing Stress

List the ways you experience stress physically, emotionally and behaviorally.

Physically	Emotionally	Behaviorally

Circle the ways stress affects you that are most troubling.

List two or three things you can do to reduce these symptoms or times when you notice these symptoms are less intensive.

My Stressed-Out List

(For Teens)

Write down things that stressed you out in the following places.
At the end, there is a question. Answer it in your diary.

My Stressed-Out list!

What are some helpful things you can do to cope with your stress?

Stress Management

(For Teens)

Complete the worksheet by answering the questions.

Stress Management

WHAT IS STRESS?

Stress happens when you have strong feelings of being worried anxious or overwhelmed!

Stress buttons or triggers are things that happen and cause you to feel stressed out.

STRESS HAPPENS WHEN YOU HAVE:

What are your top five stress buttons?

1._____
2._____
3._____
4._____
5._____

- a lot of things going on at once
- an important decision to make
- an unexpected change in your life
- a big event coming up
- something really dangerous or
- terrifying happens to you

WHERE DO YOU FEEL STRESS IN YOUR BODY?

GOOD WAYS TO COPE WITH STRESS!

Figure out your stress button.
Take a time-out from whatever is stressing you out.
Talk to an adult.
Practice relaxation to help your body calm down
Listen to music or watch a movie.
Keep a Stress Journal.
Use positive self-talk!

WHERE IS YOUR RELAXING PLACE?

_____

My Stress Management Plan

(For Teens)

Make your stress management plan using this worksheet.

My Stress Management Plan

People that who can help me:

Fun activities I can do:

What I am grateful for:

Positive statements I can say to myself:

Ways I can relax/rest:

What I am looking forward to:

Stress Management Mindful Exercises

(For Teens)

Stress affects your body, health, and energy. The stress response is meant to be fleeting. We cannot see the wider picture because stress narrows our perspective. Our focus widens as we grow more relaxed. The question then becomes: How do you unwind? By using different behaviors that not only feel happy but also put us in a calmer, more peaceful condition, where we can better handle whatever life can throw at us, we can unwind. Here are some behaviors through which a person can unwind their thoughts.

✦ Practicing Deep Breathing Techniques

We sometimes take for granted the profound emotional control that our breathing provides. Your nervous system that is responsible for your body's calming response, can be activated through breathing.

"Breathing in for a count of four, holding for that number of counts, and then exhaling for up to two times" is one of the most relaxing breathing exercises you can do. If you want to practice deep relaxation breathing, you might slightly tighten your throat and imitate the sound of the ocean.

✦ Encourage Sincere Connection

How often do we genuinely give someone our full attention? When was the last time someone was fully present in your life?

Our need to positively interact with others is in third place behind the need for food and shelter. The good news is that you may focus more attention outward and feel more connected by taking care of your wellbeing with techniques like breathing and self-compassion.

✦ Work On Showing Empathy for Others

Imagine yourself having a bad day because you have spilled your coffee on yourself, and it is pouring outside. When a friend is experiencing a genuine emergency call, you quickly get up and aid them. What happens to your mental state at that precise moment?

You suddenly have a lot of energy and are available to them. That is what happens to your life when you actively pursue altruism, help, and compassion. Many of us have discovered that it greatly improves our well-being when we carry out small deeds of kindness.

✦ Fifth Sense

You can perform this quick mindfulness exercise anywhere, at any time, and probably without anyone knowing. It is a simple method to focus on the task, awaken your attention, or fully ground yourself in the present moment. Take note of these five items as you look at yourself. For instance, I can see my computer, a couch, the cat, a novel, and some trees right now. Observe the four sounds you can hear around you right now. "I hear my fingers tapping on the keyboard, the fan, my cat howling, and footsteps coming from the flat above me". Now take a moment to notice three objects you can touch or feel. "I can feel the cushion below me, the weight of the blanket across my shoulders, and the softness of the keypad on my laptop", for example. Watch two things that you can smell right now.

"Along with the remnants of my lunch on the table next to me, I can smell some spearmint lotion on my hands". Now take time to check if there is anything you can taste right now. "I still have a faint flavor of the orange juice I have just drunk".

This little mindfulness practice is a simple, enjoyable method to increase your awareness of the sensory experiences you are having in the current moment and possibly to realize that there is more to notice and feel in each passing minute than you might initially think. This may also help you feel more grateful for each current moment's abundance.

Stress Relief Games

(For Teens)

Games are a wonderful way to relieve tension. Games have a focus that makes us entertain while keeping us in the present. Checkers, Monopoly, and Scrabble are some other strategy board games. These activities are excellent for teens, adults and children since they enhance communication and learning motivation.

Gardening

Making a garden or caring for a houseplant can be a wonderful way to get back in touch with nature, enhance your surroundings, and gain additional health advantages. Gaining more sunlight exposure, developing creativity, and upping physical activity are some of the main stress-relieving advantages of gardening. According to research, daily outdoor exposure can help lessen depressive and anxious symptoms.

Laughing

A good laugh can help you unwind and reduce tension. Laughing produces dopamine and other feel-good chemicals, distracts you from stress, and, if you laugh vigorously enough, can even give you a nice physical workout. Additionally, it puts you in a better mood, and sharing a laugh with others can strengthen relationships. You might discover more about what makes you laugh by viewing comedies on television or in movies and searching online for humorous memes or videos. While it's wonderful to laugh with loved ones, don't be afraid to laugh heartily on your own for all the stress-relieving advantages.

CHAPTER 10
DEPRESSION AND ANXIETY MANAGEMENT SKILLS

(For Teachers/Parents)

Teenagers and adults in the United States experience depression more frequently than any other mental health disease, and severe depression is classified as a mental illness on par with terminal-stage cancer. Teenagers with untreated mental illness are more likely to struggle in relationships, the workplace, and education. They are more likely to engage in unsafe sexual practices and struggle with substance abuse. Teenagers who struggle with depression are also more susceptible to getting sick physically than other teenagers.

In addition, untreated depression is the primary factor in suicide, and among those aged 10 to 24, suicide is the second greatest cause of death. You must be aware of the symptoms of depression to aid your teen.

Teenage depression symptoms could include: being depressed or sad, irritated with sketching, isolated for long-time reduced energy and weariness, inability to focus and lack motivation, suicidal ideas, variations in sleep (too much or too little), alterations in appetite, alterations in academic performance, unbearable physical symptoms (such as headaches and stomach problems) that do not improve after treatment. This chapter's aim is to develop depression and anxiety management skills in teens.

Socialize

(For Teens)

Humans cannot easily have the social component removed from their evolution because they are born into social groupings and spend their entire lives as members of society.

However, how do social interactions impact our health?

According to psychologist, direct human contact sets off sections of our neural system that generate a "cocktail" of neurotransmitters. It controls how we react to stress and anxiety. In other words, face-to-face communication with others may eventually help us become more tolerant of stressors.

Dopamine is also formed as a result of social connection, which kills pain; it's like a naturally produced morphine.

Thus, socializing with different types of people, knowing them and understanding their differences can help you in reducing anxiety and depressions symptoms.

Keep your Body and Mind Healthy

(For Teens)

As you get older, your minds and bodies go through natural changes. There are certain things you could do to assist in slowing any memory loss and reduce your risk of getting Alzheimer's or some other health issue, though.

Get Rest

Your ability to think depends on how well you sleep. Some theories contend that sleep enhances memory consolidation and improves overall memory and cognitive performance by removing aberrant proteins from the brain. It's crucial to make an effort to get seven to eight hours of uninterrupted sleep every night. Your brain needs time to successfully consolidate and successfully store memories of uninterrupted sleep. Your brain's health is negatively impacted by sleep apnea, which may also cause your inability to acquire uninterrupted hours of sleep.

Keep your Mind Engaged

Your brain is like a muscle; you must exercise it to keep it strong. You can engage in various mental exercises to keep your brain in tip-top shape, including Sudoku and crossword puzzles, reading, playing cards, and jigsaw puzzle construction. Think of it as cerebral cross-training. Therefore, mix up your tasks to boost efficiency. Last but not least, limit your television viewing because it is a passive activity that does little to stimulate your brain.

What Bugs Me?

(For Teens)

Write down things or situations in the given bugs that make you depressed or anxious. Color to show intensity of the thoughts.

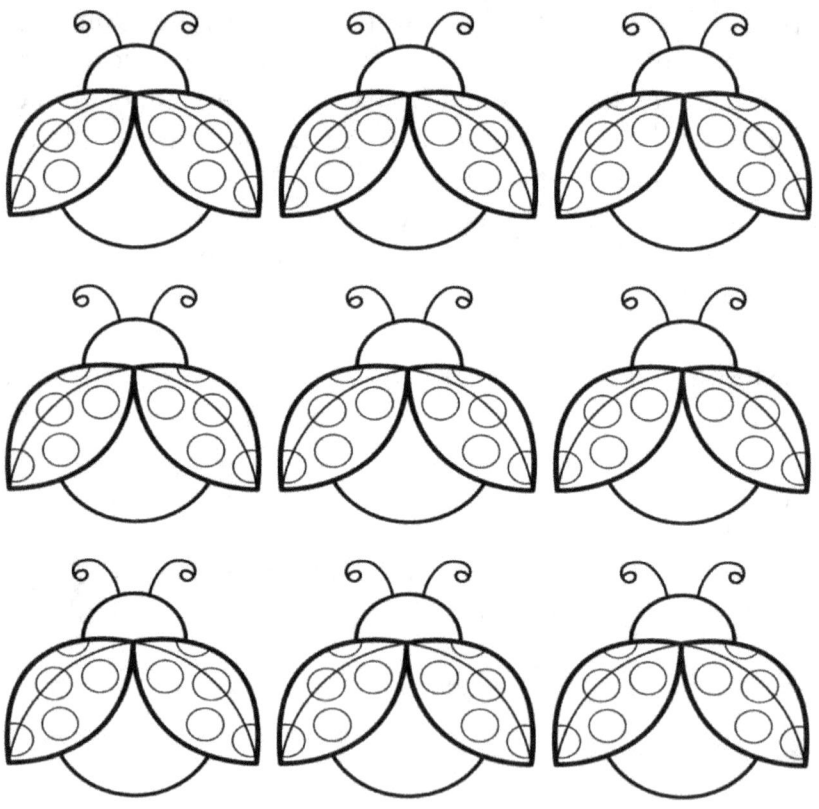

Depression and My Body

(For Teens)

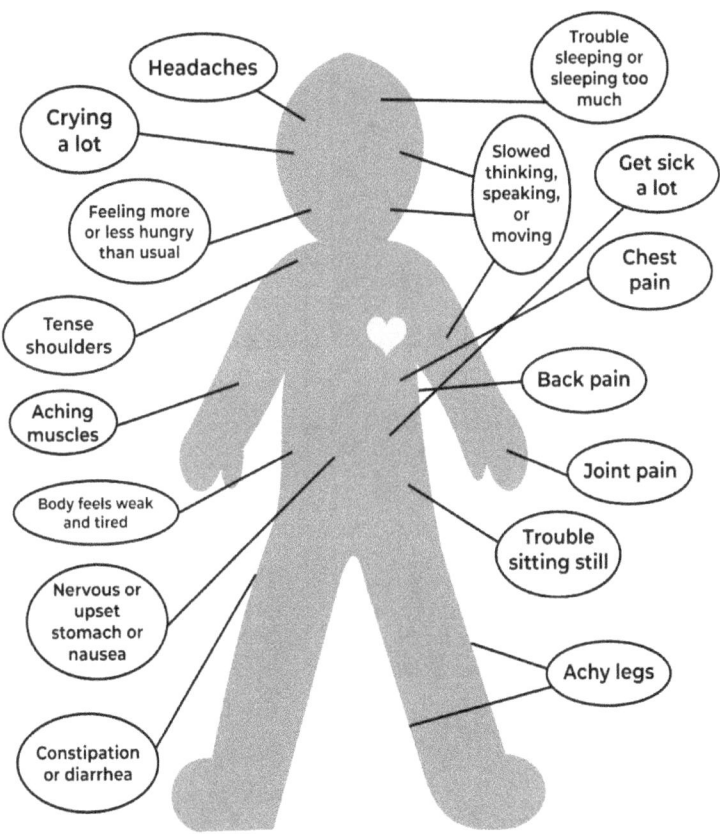

Depression Coping Plan

(For Teens)

Make your coping plan using the following worksheet.

Depression Coping Plan

Social supports:

Crisis resources:

Therapy-based tools:

Media consumption:

Stress management:

Introduction to Anxiety

(For Teens)

Use this worksheet to know what triggers your anxiety.

Introduction to Anxiety

Anxiety is the body's response to situations that are interpreted as threatening. Without any anxiety, you would probably make bad decisions, such as driving too fast on the highway, or not paying your bills. However, too much anxiety can lead to avoidance or unpleasant physical, emotional, and cognitive symptoms.

What are three things that trigger your anxiety?

1.
2.
3.

What are three physical symptoms that you experience when you feel anxious?

1.
2.
3.

What are three thoughts you tend to have when you feel anxious?

1.
2.
3.

What are three things you do to cope when you are anxious?

1.
2.
3.

Anxiety Breakdown

(For Teens)

This activity will help you to understand your anxious thoughts by breaking them down into smaller thoughts.

Anxiety Breakdown

What is making me feel anxious?

_____

What are some of the negative thoughts that I am having?

( )   ( )   ( )

How is my body responding?

_____

What is the worst thing that can happen?

_____

What do I have in my control to keep this from happening?

_____

What can I do so to calm my body down?

_____

What are positive thoughts to help calm my mind?

( )   ( )   ( )

My Anxiety Levels

(For Teens)

My Anxiety Levels

Use this worksheet to explore what happens to your body, thoughts and feelings as your anxiety increases!
Write down the helpful coping skills that you use for each level of anxiety.

LEVEL 1 What happens when you first start feeling anxious?

How do you cope?

LEVEL 2 What happens as you become more anxious?

How do you cope?

LEVEL 3 What happens when you are at your most anxious?

How do you cope?

My Social Anxiety

(For Teens)

My Social Anxiety

Social anxiety occurs wherever you start feeling nervous or scared when you are around other people. Use the worksheet to explore more about social anxiety!

What social situations make me feel anxious?

- Sitting in the lunch room
- Being on stage
- Talking in front of the class
- Meeting new people
- Talking on the phone
- Being around a lot of people
- Going to school
- People watching me
- Playing a sport
- Making eye contact
- Having a conversation
- Walking into the classroom
- Talking to adults
- Teacher calling on me
- Walking in the hallway

_____   _____

_____   _____

What thoughts do I have when I'm in a social situation?

How do I feel? (Color in)

What can I do to start coping with my social anxiety?

_____   _____

_____   _____

Therapy Games for Teens & Middle School

Anxiety vs. Truth

(For Teen)

Write down anxious thoughts on left side and truth on right side.

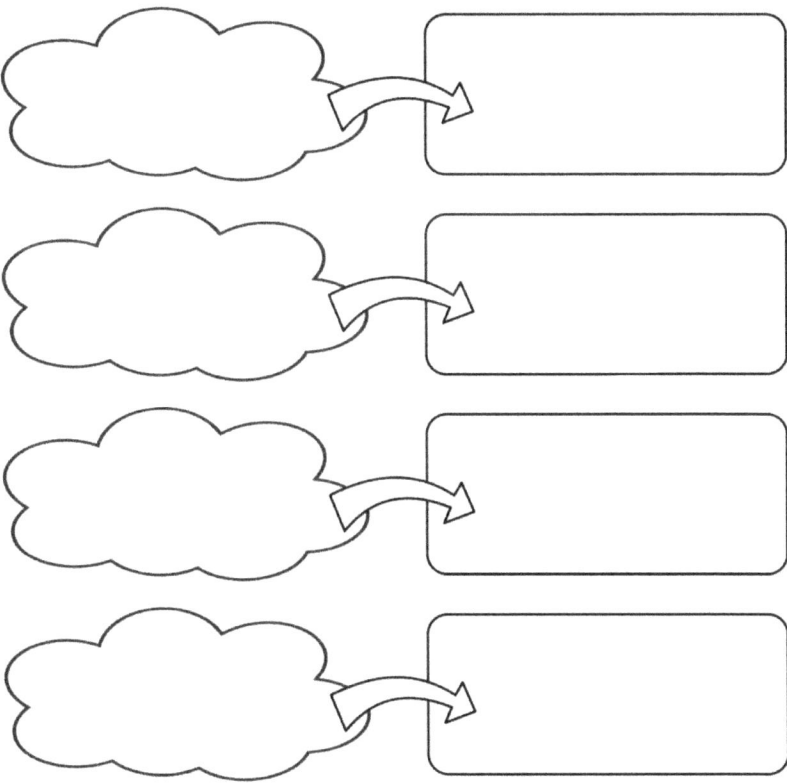

Mindfulness Exercises for Anxiety Management

(For Teens)

Being mindful involves being aware of daily life and the activities we frequently speed through. By returning to the body, you can lower the weight of your mind. You won't need to pay for an hour of classes or force your body into awkward positions, so don't worry. Likely, you already have all the resources needed to engage in mindfulness practice. These strategies incorporate brief mindfulness periods during the day to reduce anxiety and promote mental calmness.

1. Make A Resolution

Your yoga instructor asks you to establish a goal for your exercise for a reason. Establishing an intent can help you focus and remind you of why you are doing something, whether you do it in the morning notebook or before significant events. Set an intent for it if anything makes you nervous, like giving a major speech at school. Before going to the gym or before eating, you may, for instance, make a conscious effort to take care of your body.

1. Look Up

Look up at the stars instead of simply the television in front of you. Whether emptying the garbage or arriving home late, pause, take a few belly breaths, and gaze up at the sky. Let the universe serve as a reminder that life is bigger than your concerns or email.

2. Maintain Single-Minded Attention

If you use it properly, your to-do list may be a type of mindfulness. Give one task your complete and undivided attention for five minutes. No multitasking, including checking your phone, clicking notifications, or browsing the internet should be practiced. Until the timer runs off, let that one task take center stage.

3. Don't Use Your Phone

Do you need to carry your phone when you enter the other room? When do you use the restroom? Do you eat when you sit down? Put your phone away in another room. Sit down and take a deep breath before you begin to eat rather than stressing over it. In the restroom, give yourself some time to tend to your requirements. When you're through, your phone will still be there.

Mindfulness Exercises for Depression Management

(For Teens)

✤ Mindful Breathing Technique

The breath is where mindfulness exercises begin. Short, laborious breaths can be symptoms of anxiety and panic brought on by unwanted or unpleasant thoughts. Deeper breathing happens in the abdomen, whereas anxious breathing happens in the chest. Slowing your breath, bringing your heart rate back to a steady rhythm, and using grounding techniques will help you feel less anxious due to unsettling thoughts.

Use this mindful breathing technique when feeling nervous or panicked to help you stay in the present.

- Find a peaceful area where you can concentrate on breathing without interruptions before you start. Place your head over your heart and your heart over your pelvis while sitting or standing straight. If you feel you need more profound relaxation, you might choose to close your eyes before you start.
- Take a four-second nasal breather. Instead of taking a huge gulp of air, breathe in a steady, even breath. Don't hurry.
- Take a moment to hold your breath at the peak before continuing.
- Spend four seconds slowly exhaling through your nostrils. Exhale slowly and deliberately for the full four seconds rather than letting your breath out all at once.
- Repeat after a little pause at the end of your exhalation.
- Repeat the previous steps while taking another inhalation through your nose.

When you feel a change in your body and mind, keep breathing in this manner.

✤ The Five Senses Grounding Method

Practice the above mindful breathing exercise two or three times before starting this exercise to start calming your body and mind.

- Take a look around your nearby area.
- What five things can you see? Simple examples include a bird, a table, or a pencil.
- Identify four things that you can touch. This may be something like a cushion, the grass, or your hair.
- Cite three audible items. Make sure to identify any outside noises, such as a dog barking or a car driving by.
- Give the names of two smells. Consider your perfume or the neighboring flowers and plants.
- Give us a taste you can describe. It can be gum or coffee.

CHAPTER 11
ANGER AND MOOD DISORDERS MANAGEMENT SKILLS

(For Teens)

We all understand the anger and have experienced it at some point, whether it was a little annoyance or full-blown wrath. Anger is an entirely typical and usually positive human emotion. But when it spirals out of control and becomes destructive, it can cause issues—problems at work, issues in your relations, issues with your life's general quality.

Anger management aims to lessen the physiological discomfort that it creates and disturbs the emotional feelings. You cannot change, ignore, or eliminate the things or people who irritate you, but you can learn to control your moods. Consider using these activities to acquire better-coping strategies if you believe your anger is truly out of control, affecting your mood, causing mood disorders and disturbing other significant aspects of your life.

(For Teens)

Aim for Regulation, Not Repression

Make sure you aren't just brushing your emotions under the rug while trying to control them. It's important to strike a balance between having too many feelings and having none for healthy emotional expression.

Identify What You're Feeling

You may start taking control back by taking a minute to check in with your mood. Let's say you've been going out with someone for a while. You attempted to set up a date with them last week, but they declined. You contacted again yesterday with the message, "I'd want to see you soon. All of a sudden, you're quite upset. You fling your phone out the window, tip your trash can over, and kick your desk, stabbing your toe without pausing to think.

Ask yourself, "What am I feeling at this moment?" What has happened to cause me to feel this way? (Disappointed, perplexed, outraged) (They ignored me without explaining.)

Does there any alternate explanation exist for the circumstance that would make sense? (Perhaps they're under stress, ill, or coping with another issue they don't feel comfortable disclosing. They may provide further details when they can.)

What do I want to do in response to these emotions? (Scream, toss things in anger, and send an offensive text back.)

Is there a more effective method of handling them? (Ask if all is well. Question their next availability. Take a stroll or a run.)

You can change your first extreme response by reframing your thinking to consider potential alternatives. It could take some time before this reaction becomes ingrained in you. Practice will make it simpler to do these actions mentally.

Accept Your Emotions

Try to downplay your emotions to yourself if you want to improve your ability to control your emotions. You can become more at ease with your emotions if you accept them. You may feel intense emotions more thoroughly and avoid extreme, counterproductive reactions by increasing your comfort level with them.

Try viewing emotions as messengers to practice accepting them. They are neither nice nor bad. They are impartial. Even if they occasionally trigger unpleasant emotions, they still provide useful information.

Try this as an example: "I'm frustrated because I keep misplacing my keys, which causes me to be late". To help me remember to leave them in the same spot, I should put a bowl on the shelf by the door. Accepting emotions may improve life's happiness and reduce symptoms of mental illness. Additionally, thinking of one's emotions to be constructive may result in better happiness levels.

Give Yourself Some Space

Separating yourself from strong emotions can help you ensure that you're responding to them rationally, such as leaving a distressing place, could be this separation. But by diverting your attention, you can also establish some mental distance.

It's not healthy to completely block or avoid feelings, but it's also okay to divert your attention from them until you're in a better position to deal with them. Just be sure to visit them again. Healthy diversion only lasts for a short time. Consider going for a stroll, viewing a fun video, speaking with a loved one, or spending time with your pet.

Anger Map

(For Teens)

Answer the following questions to construct your anger map.

What kind of face do you have when you are angry?

What things do you say?

How do you behave when you're angry?

What happens to your body when you're angry?

Other ways of handing your anger

What could your anger help you to achieve?

Have you learnt anything about your anger?

What helps when you're angry

My Anger Triggers

(For Teens)

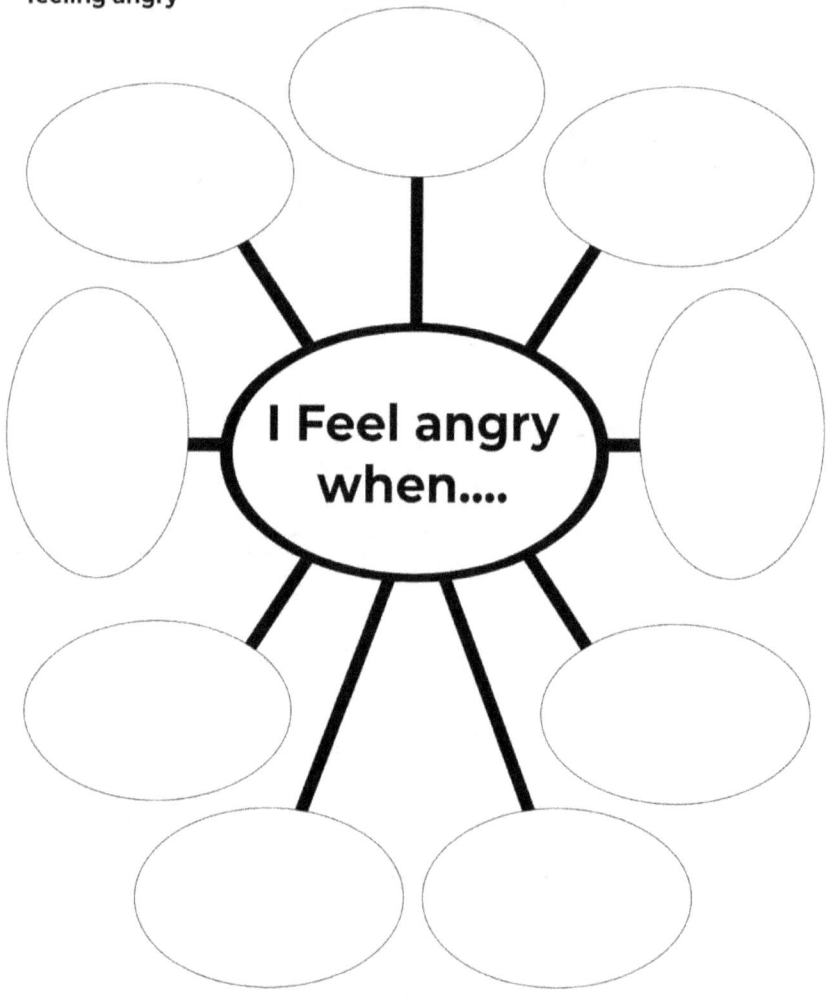

Anger Exploration

(For Teens)

ANGER EXPLORATION WORKSHEET

Use this worksheet to explore and discuss a recent anger episode!

What happened that made me feel angry?

_____

_____

What other feelings did I experience?

- ☐ sad
- ☐ annoyed
- ☐ guilty
- ☐ _____
- ☐ worried
- ☐ scared
- ☐ stressed
- ☐ _____
- ☐ jealous
- ☐ lonely
- ☐ embarrassed
- ☐ _____

What thoughts went through my head?

_____

_____

How did I respond?

- ☐ yelling and screaming
- ☐ name-caling
- ☐ crying

What ended up happening?

_____

_____

What was my consequence?

_____

_____

What can I do differently next time if this situation happens again?

- ☐ use on I-Feel Message
- ☐ deep breathing
- ☐ _____
- ☐ walk away
- ☐ tell an adult
- ☐ _____
- ☐ count to ten
- ☐ distract myself
- ☐ _____

I Feel Mad Today

(For Teens)

I FEEL MAD TODAY!

Answer these questions to help you explore your feelings of anger today.

What happened to make you feel mad?
_____
_____
_____

What other feelings are you experiencing?
_____   _____   _____

How long have you been feeling this way? _____

What has happened to make it better? _____
_____

What has happened to make it worse? _____
_____

What do you need right now? _____
_____

What can you do to start feeling better?

(1) _____   (2) _____

(3) _____   (4) _____

Anger Journal

(For Teens)

What made me feel angry? (Anger Trigger)

What other feelings did I experience?

How did I handle it? (Coping Skill)

What ended up happening? What was my consequence?

What should I do differently next time?

How Anger Feels

(For Teens)

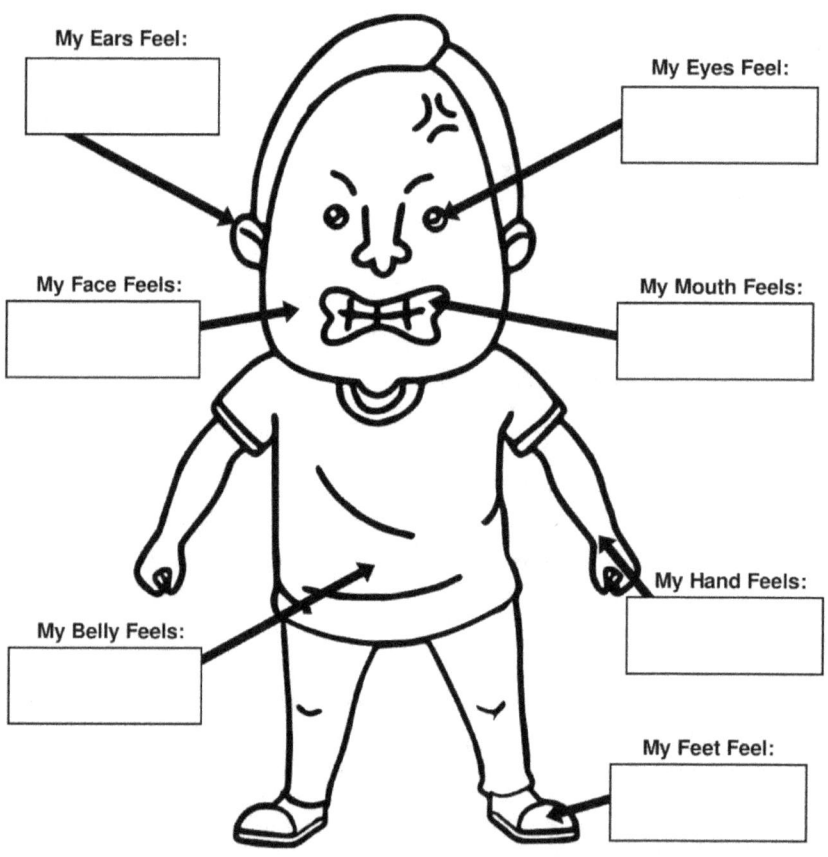

Anger Meter

(For Teens)

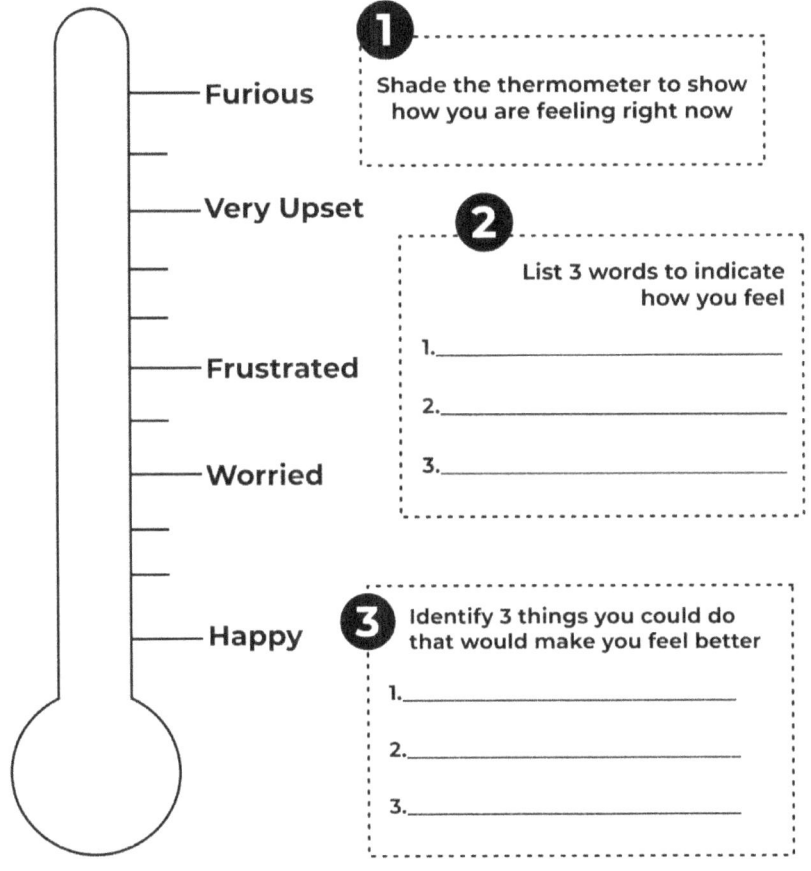

When I Feel Angry

(For Teens)

WHEN I FEEL ANGRY

I THINK....(What are some thoughts that go through your head whenever you feel angry?)

I SAY....(What are some things you say to others whenever you feel angry?)

I DO....(What are some behaviors you display whenever you feel angry?)

_____   _____

_____   _____

_____   _____

What are some things you can think, say or do instead?

Feeling Zones

(For Teens)

Identify your feeling zone by looking at colors and emotions inside them.

Feeling Zones

Blue Zone	Green Zone	Yellow Zone	Red Zone
sad tired sick moving tired slowly	happy calm feeling ok focused ready to learn	frustrated worried silly/wiggly excited loss of some control	mad/angry terrified yelling/hitting elated out of control

What are you Feeling Today?

(For Teens)

When I Feel Sad

(For Teens)

WHEN I FEEL SAD

I THINK....
(What are some thoughts that go through your head whenever you feel sad?)

I SAY....
(What are some things you say to other whenever you feel sad?)

I DO....
(What behavior do you display whenever you feel sad?)

_____   _____

_____   _____

My Emotions Wheel

(For Teens)

Draw and color emotions with the given words. Write one coping skill at the back of each emotion. Cut and spin whenever you feel sad. Use coping skill to feel good.

My Emotions Wheel

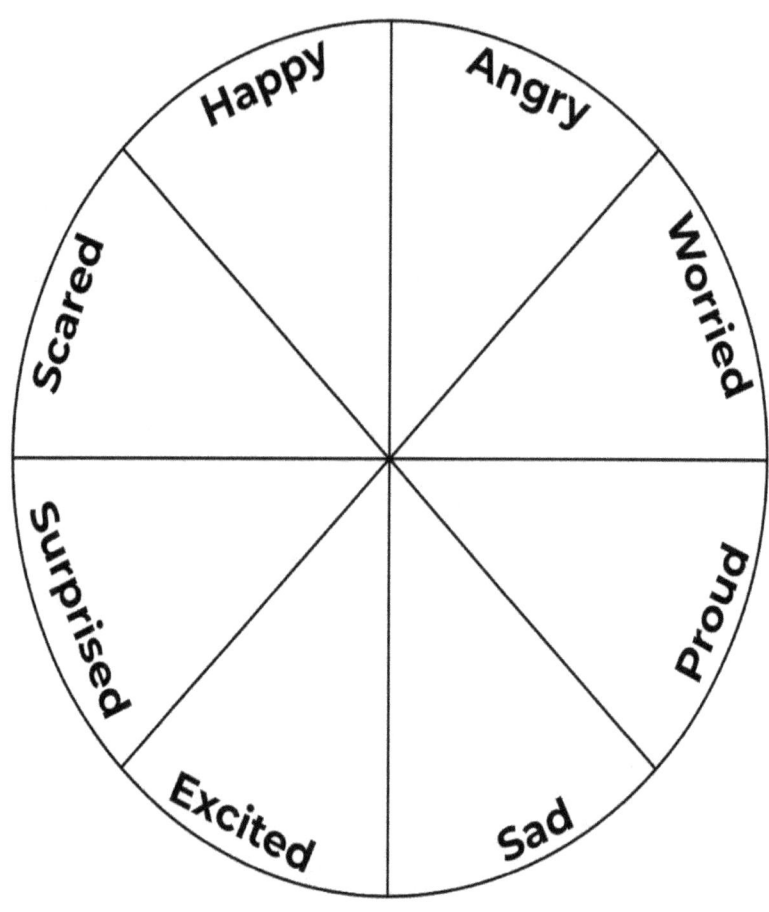

Mindful Exercises

(For Teens)

Teen's meditation is one of the most popular and well-known mindfulness practices. Meditation can be quite easy, even though it might appear esoteric or difficult. The goal of these activities is to turn ordinary experiences into specific ones.

- **Walking Introspection**

The practice of meditation while walking, usually in a straight line or circle, is precisely what it sounds like. You can do it practically at anyplace, whether you're strolling around the neighborhood, going to the park with your friends, or walking to work.

- **Single-Tasking**

Single-tasking is the antithesis of multitasking, as you probably already know. All you have to do is commit yourself entirely to the task at hand. Concentrate on one job at a time when using a computer. Close all the browser tabs that aren't related to the project you're working on; despite how much you might not want to. Doing so can help clear your mind and possibly develop laser-like focus.

- **Conscious Eating**

A few simple mindful eating techniques, such as paying attention to the sizzling of your food in the pan and chewing carefully to appreciate each bite, can help you make mealtimes more thoughtful. Try and eat with your non-dominant hand, among other mindful eating suggestions. Focus on your food's flavors, scents, and textures during the first few minutes of your meal while eating in silence. While you dine, turn off your television and keep your phone away.

Mood Lifting Games

(For Parents/Teachers)

↓ Wiggle and Freeze Game

With movement, this game can help teens develop their awareness of physical sensations and begin practicing mindfulness. You must wiggle, move, shake, stomp, or dance until you command, "Freeze!" Encourage kids to focus closely on the bodily sensations they sense as soon as everyone stops moving. This game may be played repeatedly; you can even play music and pause it when it's time to freeze.

↓ Monkey See Monkey Do

Teens can play this excellent mindfulness game to develop their body awareness and consider how they move through space. Take up the role of the monkey as the adult, and guide the participants through various positions. Try to change how you carry your weight by standing on one foot, going down on all or raising one foot in the air. Find out from the children how each posture feels. Does it require a lot of balance, or does it stretch them out greatly? Let it be absurd. When children move about, giggles are likely to follow. Simply accept it. Ask the children to observe how their breath changes as they laugh.

↓ Dragon Breathing

Teens can learn to breathe deeply and slowly by practicing dragon breathing. The basic version doesn't need any materials, but you might add a fun project to emphasize the point. To maximize the enjoyment, read or make up a quick dragon narrative to get everyone's creativity going.

- Tell the children to inhale deeply, filling their chest and belly.
- When they're prepared, tell them to take a deep breath and "breathe out their fire."

It can be amusing to watch the papers blow as the children exhale if you have a paper on hand.

✤ Calm Cards

Little reminders can occasionally assist individuals in cultivating mindfulness during trying situations. This is another simple activity that gives youngsters a practical item to use every day.

- Encourage the children to consider what they can do to relax, such as drinking water, taking deep breaths, shutting their eyes, reading books, or hugging a buddy.
- After that, ask them to illustrate each activity on separate cards. They can also be given printed images to paste.
- Have the children labeled the cards if they can write? Punch holes in the cards, then bind them using yarn or a book ring.
- When children are agitated, angry, terrified, or sad, they can use the cards to help them control their emotions and feel good.

CHAPTER 12: WORRY AND FEAR MANAGEMENT SKILLS

(For Teens)

Facing your fear is the only way to overcome it. Avoiding our concerns doesn't help us move forward; it just makes us nervous. However, be kind to yourself and only act in ways that seem secure to you. If you realize your anxiety is increasing, pause and look for anything relaxing or consoling to see or do. You can attempt to explore your fear once more, taking breaks as necessary if it feels safe later. It's important to keep in mind that therapists can be quite helpful in helping you work through avoidance techniques if you find it difficult to deal with persistent anxieties. Working with a therapist to establish a safe space where you may face your anxiety and reconstruct your memories is especially crucial if you have experienced trauma. But you can also try mindfulness meditation if you want your fear or anxiety more manageable.

Find out more about mindfulness practices, activities and exercises related to fear and worry in this chapter. All you have to do is to sit quietly and focus on the now. Recognize dread or anxiety when it manifests. Attempt to be curious. Take note of the fear. Observe how it makes you feel physical. Take note of any related thoughts. Instead of getting caught up in the narrative or attempting to change it, try to observe it as it is. And when you need to, stop and focus on anything unimportant, like your breath or your hands in your lap. Be aware that it may be beneficial to stop, open your eyes, and examine the objects in the room if you feel upset to be curious or take a short stroll. Try the strategies given in this chapter and solve worksheets to overcome your fears and worries.

(For Teens)

Stay in the Present Moment

People spend too much time hoping for happiness in the future rather than appreciating the moment they are in right now. Life is finite. Thus, these people will eventually look back and discover that they have wasted their entire lives anticipating the future rather than appreciating the present they were given. Consider using these suggestions if you want to make the most of the present and savor each moment that comes your way.

- **Decide to Stay Present**

There will be some work and commitment involved in staying in the present. Spend a few minutes every morning telling yourself to appreciate the day for what it is and to make the most of it.

- **Establish A System**

The next step is to create a strategy for reminding oneself to stay in the present. This could involve setting a note on your phone to remind you to be in the present or scheduling a little time each day when you just think about the present.

Take Small Acts of Bravery

In the short run, avoiding your nervous triggers can help, but it can make your worries worse over time. Try taking even a modest step toward something that makes you worry. The key to overcoming worry is realizing that, even if what you fear, does occur but you will be able to handle it.

Your thoughts and feelings are connected. When you're worried, you could exaggerate how dangerous something is while also underestimating your capacity to handle it. Instead of assuming the worst when faced with an uncertain circumstance, consider alternative interpretations. Consider the evidence for and against the veracity of your hypothesis.

Plan Worry Time

Take some time to feed your fears because it's difficult to stop worrying completely. You can prevent your anxieties from taking over other times by taking even 10 to 15 minutes each night to jot them down or go through them in your brain. Learn about your worries. Record the finest and worst times in a diary. To proactively manage your worries, identify the trends and plan for your week or day.

My Top 5 Worries

(For Teens)

Write down your top five worries in the given clouds.

My Top Five Worries

My Worry Clouds

(For Teens)

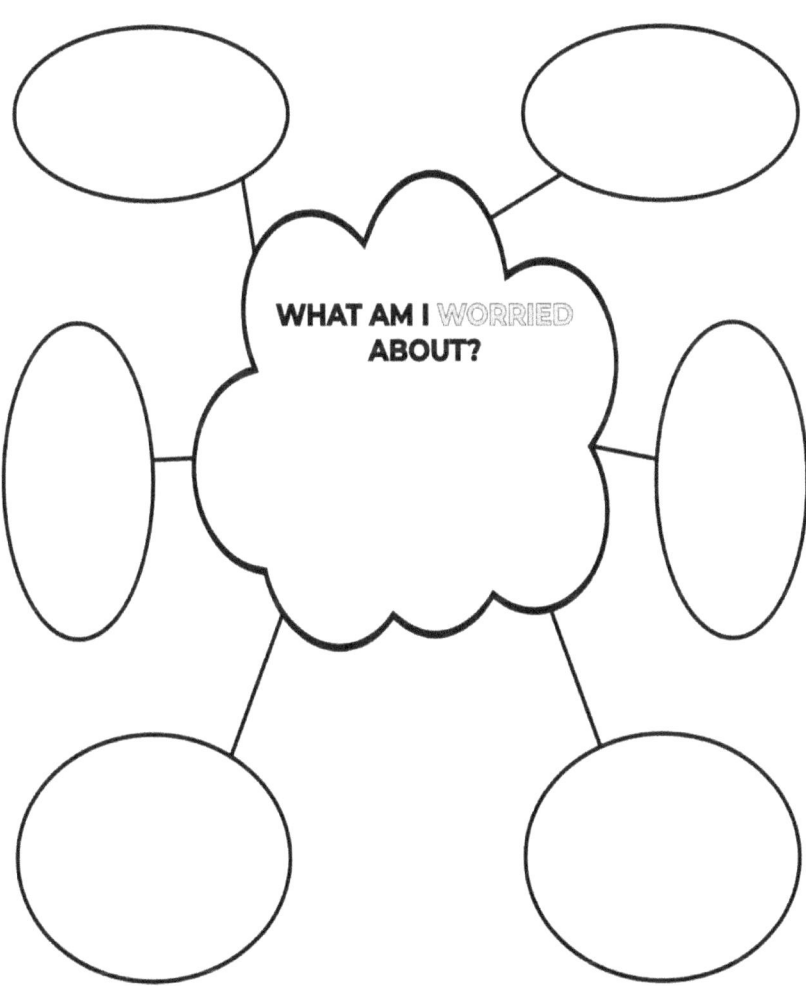

A Peek Inside My Mind

(For Teens)

A PEEK INSIDE MY MIND

In these clouds, write down all of your thoughts and feelings that you are having. They can be happy thoughts, sad thoughts, worried thoughts, excited thoughts!

Facing Fears

(For Teens)

Facing Your Fears

If we overcome our fears, it can help us to build our confidence gradually. You can think of it as being like climbing the steps of a ladder.

Start by writing down the fear that you are facing. Then for each step of the ladder, write down one thing you can do to face that fear head-on. Make sure to reward yourself for each step you take.

The fear I am facing is:_____

Therapy Games for Teens & Middle School

Getting to Know My Emotions

(For Teens)

There are some emotions given in the left column. Think of a situation related to them and write answer in other columns.

Inside Out: Getting to Know My Emotions

My emotion	Feels like	Sounds Like	A memory when I felt...
Sadness			
Disgust			
Joy			
Anger			
Fear			

My Fears

(For Teens)

My Fears

What are some things that make you feel nervous or scared?

What do you think about when you are nervous or scared?

How does your body feel when you are nervous or scared?
Color the areas where you can sense these feelings

What's something you can do to feel better next time you are afraid?

Fear Crushing

(For Teens)

This time, think of only your biggest fear and crush it through this worksheet.

Fear Crushing Worksheet

My Core Fear

Break down the fear into manageable parts

How can / will I challenge that fear?

I'll repeat this affirmation when I'm facing my fear

I want to accomplish this more than I am scared of it

I'll use these resources to crush my fear

Overcoming Fear Questionnaire

(For Teens)

Tell me your thoughts about overcoming fear. Choose true or false for the given statements.

- Fear can be a useful thing.

　　　　　　　　　　True　　　　False

- If you don't face your fears you might not accomplish things you want to do.

　　　　　　　　　　True　　　　False

- Having fears and conquering them will lower your confidence

　　　　　　　　　　True　　　　False

- Your mental health will always be well if you fear.

　　　　　　　　　　True　　　　False

- Fear comes from the right side of the brain.

　　　　　　　　　　True　　　　False

- Fear can save us from real danger.

　　　　　　　　　　True　　　　False

Mindfulness Exercise

(For Teens)

- Sit in a comfortable position to start. Observe your breathing.
- Continue to examine your body, noting any tight spots attentively. Consider something that makes you feel tight or anxious. Spend a minute or two doing this.
- Check to see if you can make your body's tension expand now that you've caused it. You can accomplish this by concentrating on the tightness in your body or by continuing to visualize the thought, emotion, or image that makes you anxious.
- To practice handling anxiety, infuse yourself with as much of it as possible.
- Find out if you can endure this high level of anxiety for ten minutes.
- After experiencing this tension, refocus on your breath and physical awareness to reduce your anxiousness.

Learning how to sit with anxiety and fear in the present moment can be a challenging and drawn-out process. Remind yourself that worthwhile, essential things frequently require time and effort. Imagine for a moment that fear and anxiety no longer paralyze you or cause you to feel disconnected from the world. Remember that while frightening occurrences in life are unavoidable, how you react to them is entirely up to you.

PART-IV

DEVELOPING COPING SKILLS

(For Teens, Parents and Teachers)

Coping is the effort we put forth to deal with situations we have identified as potentially dangerous or stressful. Those who can adapt their answers to a scenario using a variety of coping mechanisms are the greatest at coping. Copers have an optimistic mindset and employ their abilities to achieve the greatest result. Copers are not powerless and apathetic. They seek means of gaining control over their lives.

Being a cop requires expertise in:

- Stress reduction
- Management of time
- Problem-solving
- Decision-making
- Lifestyle control

The last part of this book will focus on the coping strategies that are important and prove beneficial for kids of all ages. Move forward to learn the best coping techniques.

CHAPTER 13
COPING SKILLS WORKSHEETS AND ACTIVITIES

(For Teens, Parents and Teachers)

Enhancing or improving our resilience is another method we may make our coping strategies better. According to the American Psychological Association (APA), resilience is the ability to cope effectively with challenges such as trauma, threats, and hardship. In today's hectic world, caring for a loved one for a prolonged period or functioning as a skilled caregiver can be a substantial source of stress. We don't all naturally possess resilience, but anyone may learn how to cultivate it.

The APA states that while several factors influence resilience, having loving and dependable relationships that foster love and trust is crucial. Other elements linked to resilience include:

- Ability to create and carry out practical plans
- A favorable self-perception
- Having faith in your skills and abilities.
- Skills in problem-solving and communication
- Ability to control intense emotions and impulsive behavior

So, don't wait more and learn coping strategies with games and brain teasers.

Developing Coping Skills/Resilience

(For Teens)

Identify Connections. Maintain strong bonds with your immediate family and close friends; accept support and assistance from people who care about you. Participate actively in civic, religious, and other local groups and aid those in need.

Refrain from viewing crises as intractable issues. Try to imagine how things might be different in the future. Keep track of tiny changes in how you may already feel more optimistic as you manage challenging situations.

Recognize that life is full of change. Try to be more adaptable and recognize that you might no longer be able to achieve all of your goals. You might be able to concentrate more on the circumstances you can alter if you learn to accept situations that cannot be changed.

Approach your objective. Create attainable objectives and break them down into smaller, more manageable ones. Aim to make at least a little progress toward your goal(s) each day.

Take determined action. Take action as quickly as you can in difficult circumstances. Instead of ignoring issues and hoping they would go away, take action.

Look for chances to **learn more about yourself**. Examine how you have evolved and how you have handled your difficult experiences. Reframe them. People who have gone through disasters and severe personal adversity frequently claim better relationships, a stronger sense of self, an elevation in self-worth, a deeper spirituality, and greater respect for life.

Maintain a positive self-image. Develop self-assurance in your problem-solving skills and faith in your gut.

Observe the bigger picture. Try to have a long-term perspective and analyze your stressful situations in a larger context. Be careful not to exaggerate bad incidents.

Keep a positive mindset. Instead of obsessing about what you fear, try envisioning what you want. A positive mindset enables you to anticipate positive outcomes in life.

Ensure your wellbeing. Be mindful of your requirements and emotions. Engage in calming and entertaining activities, such as hobbies, entertainment, and exercise.

Coping Skills Bingo

(For Teens)

Choose a random number and open this bingo, start counting from up to down or left to right. Mark the skill that you get after counting to the number you have chosen. Try the skill to calm your mind.

Coping Skills

Play games on iPAD	Take space	Count to 10	Think about happy memories	Talk to a friend
Talk to Mom or Dad	Stress balls	Play cards	Dance	Take a bath or shower
Exercise	Drawing	FREE SPACE!	Write in a journal	Arts and Crafts
Watch TV	Help a friend	Painting	Think about loved ones	Watch a movie
Take a walk	Deep breathing	Listen to music	Read	Go outside

Picking Good Coping Skills

(For Teens)

Coping Skills Challenges

(For Teens)

Coping Skills CHALLENGE

4 Coping skills I'm going to try this year

1. _____
2. _____
3. _____
4. _____

3 Challenges I might face this year.

1. _____
2. _____
3. _____

2 People that will help me if I need it.

1. _____
2. _____

1 Person Responsible for the behavior

1. _____

If I Didn't Care

(For Teens)

If I Didn't Care....

If you didn't care what other people thought or said about you, what are some things you would do differently than you are doing now?

I would_____

I would not_____

I would listen to_____

I would try_____

I would_____

I would no longer_____

I would go_____

I would_____

I would say_____

I would start_____

I would_____

I would watch_____

I would stop_____

Coping Skills Brainstorm

(For Teens)

COPING SKILL BRAINSTORM

COPING SKILLS I ALREADY USE

- _____
- _____
- _____
- _____
- _____

COPING SKILLS I WOULD LIKE TO USE MORE

- _____
- _____
- _____
- _____
- _____

COPING SKILLS THAT ARE UNHEALTHY

- _____
- _____
- _____

Coping Skills Assessment

(For Teens)

COPING SKILLS ASSESSMENT

Color in how often you use each of these positive or negative coping skills to cope with your feelings!

	ALWAYS	SOMETIMES	NEVER
Use my words to hurt other people's feelings	☐	☐	☐
Take a "TIME-OUT" from the situation	☐	☐	☐
Use my body to hurt others (Hit, Bite, Kick, Push)	☐	☐	☐
Yell and Scream	☐	☐	☐
Do deep breathing or count to ten	☐	☐	☐
Make threats or look threatening	☐	☐	☐
Talk to a friend or sibling about my feelings	☐	☐	☐
Talk to an adult about my feelings	☐	☐	☐
Name-Call or insult others	☐	☐	☐
Hurt myself	☐	☐	☐
Express my feelings in a positive way	☐	☐	☐
Find something to distract me	☐	☐	☐
Throw objects	☐	☐	☐
Cry	☐	☐	☐
Use bad words or swear/cuss	☐	☐	☐

Coping Skills Anywhere

(For Teens)

Coping ANYWHERE!

Triggers can happen anywhere! There are situations that occur at home, school or in the community that can make you angry or anxious. Some coping skills can only be used in certain locations. For example, *"go to my room"* can only be done at home. Each location might require different coping skills in order to handle the situation in the best way. Use this worksheet to come up with helpful coping skills you can use in each of these environments!

COPING SKILLS THAT I CAN USE AT HOME!

_____   _____

_____   _____

_____   _____

COPING SKILLS THAT I CAN USE AT SCHOOL!

_____   _____

_____   _____

_____   _____

COPING SKILLS THAT I CAN USE AT COMMUNITY!

_____   _____

_____   _____

_____   _____

I Can Cope

(For Teens)

I Can Cope! with feeling ANXIOUS

Some things that make me feel anxious are……

1. _____
2. _____
3. _____

These changes happen when I feel anxious:

Changes in my body…	Thoughts I have…	Things I do…

When I feel anxious, I can cope by:

Check all of the coping skills that might be helpful! Use the blank spaces to write in your own

- ☐ Deep breathing
- ☐ Using positive self-talk
- ☐ Meditating or relaxing
- ☐ Talking to a friend
- ☐ Talking to an adult
- ☐ Playing a game

- ☐ Going to walk
- ☐ Writing in my journal
- ☐ Practicing mindfulness
- ☐ Thinking happy thoughts
- ☐ Keeping myself busy
- ☐ Exercising

- _____
- _____
- _____
- _____
- _____
- _____

Coping with Feelings

(For Teens)

Coping with Feelings

Use this worksheet to come up with coping skills for the different feelings below!

When I'm feeling [angry face] I can _____

Something that makes me feel angry is _____

When I'm feeling [sad face] I can _____

Something that makes me feel sad is _____

When I'm feeling [scared face] I can _____

Something that makes me feel scared is _____

When I'm feeling [hurt face] I can _____

Something that makes me feel hurt is _____

When I'm feeling [worried face] I can _____

Something that makes me feel worried is _____

Roll a Coping Skill

(For Teens)

ROLL A COPING SKILL

Roll the dice and look at all the coping skills in that row. Then color code each coping skill based on the colors you choose for the following options:

☐ This coping skill gets me into trouble often

☐ Sometimes this coping is a problem for me

☐ I don't use this skill to cope

Sleep all day	Do drugs or alcohol	Hurt others	Blaming yourself	All or nothing thinking	Slamming doors
Not eat	Make bad choices	Destroy things	Not trying at all or quitting	Gossiping	Procrastination
Overeat	Throw things	Say mean things	Hurtful self talk	Lying	Shut down completely
Cursing	Refusing to talk to anyone	Threaten others	Bullying others	Catastrophizing	Bottle up emotions
Avoiding the problem	Hurt yourself	Yell and scream	Denying	Throwing a tantrum	Blaming others
⚀	⚁	⚂	⚃	⚄	⚅

Coping Skill Wheel

(For Teens)

Spin and choose.

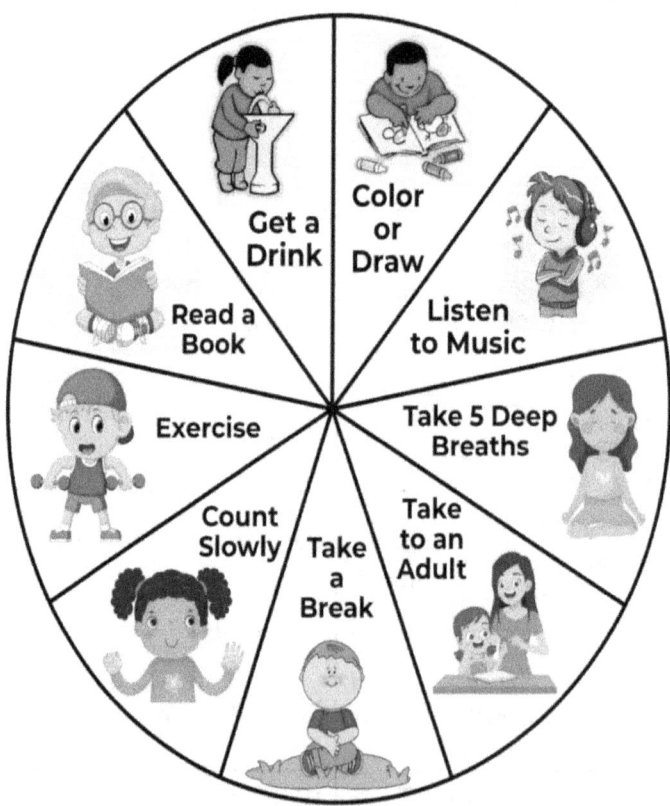

Coping Skill Word Search Game

(For Teens)

Can you find the words?

Coping Skills

```
A K U C E Z D E M Q U D P E I H J
P P T Z R O E J Q X U Q P E F E M
P L L D W C O P I N G S K I L L S
L L E V E W A O Q C X N O M R Y T
A I C K X L G D H W V Y H T S C B
Y S L G E X F J N R W V W A C O S
W T Z O R D X T F I A R N L J L P
I E I Z C W C R W T L W D K R O R
T N H K I M O E F E K S Z T Y R E
H T Y O S E O P Y A A J M O B H A
Y O H F E D C N W N W O C S R S D
O M E F N I M L C O A U L O E Q A
U U G Q Y T B A B T Y R N M A X B
R S V Z X A V G P E J N V E T P O
P I A W A T C H T V U A X O H P O
E C F R T E J L E H M L C N E A K
T A K E A N A P T G A R D E N I Z
```

Meditate	Write a note	Talk to someone
Breathe	Garden	Listen to music
Read a book	Exercise	Take a nap
Play with your pet	Watch TV	Color
Journal	Walk away	Coping skills

I am Lucky

(For Teens)

Now you have already made a plan for coping skills. It is time to appreciate your effort and remind yourself that you have now arranged all strategies that you are going to use in future. Use this worksheet.

I am  Lucky to have a wealth of coping skills

If I feel: I can cope by.....

If I feel:	I can cope by.....
Sad	
Frustrated	
Bored	
Angry	
Hyper	
Discouraged	

Coping Skills= positive strategies to help me deal with tough feelings and situations

The End Note

Every parent wants the best for their kids in life, and by that, we don't just mean having a nice career and a best result, but also making them happy. All parents are concerned about how they might facilitate that.

It's more important to develop a basic set of abilities that enable people to deal with life's inevitable obstacles, than to focus on academic performance and extracurricular activities. All of these competencies fall under the category of executive function abilities, which we employ for self-regulation. The majority of successful and contented persons have good executive function abilities.

Every stage of life requires the development of life skills. Teenagers must prepare for adulthood like toddlers need to develop their gross motor abilities. The skills discussed in the book operate under the principle that "we feel good about ourselves when we undertake positive actions" in our Thoughts, Actions, and Feelings Circle. As a result, these skills develop settings that maintain a positive cycle. This book offers comprehensive and integrated planners and solutions to provide you with all the required assistance regarding your teen skills development.

Life is already difficult enough, but we can make it more bearable. **Therapy Games for Teens and Middle School** has all the resources needed to provide teachers and parents with what they need to help teens develop resilience. If this book has helped you as a parent or teacher, don't forget to leave feedback in comment section of **AMAZON**.

www.ingramcontent.com/pod-product-compliance
Lightning Source LLC
Chambersburg PA
CBHW072048110526
44590CB00018B/3083